1,001
PROMISES
of
God

Compiled by Linda Hang.

Print ISBN 978-1-68322-168-5

All scripture quotations are taken from the King James Version of the Bible.

Published by Barbour Books, an imprint of Barbour Publishing, Inc., P.O. Box 719, Uhrichsville, Ohio 44683, www.barbourbooks.com

Our mission is to publish and distribute inspirational products offering exceptional value and biblical encouragement to the masses.

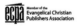

Member of the
Evangelical Christian
Publishers Association

Printed in the United States of America.

1,001
PROMISES
of
God

BARBOUR BOOKS
An Imprint of Barbour Publishing, Inc.

INTRODUCTION

It's often easy to get weighed down with the disappointments and challenges of life. Without realizing it, our hearts become heavy and our hope for a fulfilling life turns sour.

In His kindness, God has provided uplifting promises of help and encouragement for His children within the pages of His Word, the Bible. Whatever our needs, we can find in scripture the principles we need to address the issues we face.

This collection of 1,001 of scripture's most encouraging promises is the perfect everyday pick-me-up. This book is not intended to replace regular, personal Bible study. It is, however, a quick guide to hundreds of the most uplifting scriptures in the Bible. We hope it will be an encouragement to you as you read.

1

The LORD is nigh unto them that are of a broken heart;
and saveth such as be of a contrite spirit.
PSALM 34:18

2

There remaineth therefore a rest to the people of God.
For he that is entered into his rest, he also hath ceased
from his own works, as God did from his.
HEBREWS 4:9–10

3

The bows of the mighty men are broken,
and they that stumbled are girded with strength.
1 SAMUEL 2:4

4

And they rose early in the morning, and went forth into the
wilderness of Tekoa: and as they went forth, Jehoshaphat
stood and said, Hear me, O Judah, and ye inhabitants of
Jerusalem; Believe in the LORD your God, so shall ye be
established; believe his prophets, so shall ye prosper.
2 CHRONICLES 20:20

5

In the beginning was the Word, and the Word
was with God, and the Word was God.
JOHN 1:1

6

*And blessed is she that believed: for there shall
be a performance of those things which were
told her from the Lord.*

LUKE 1:45

7

*For I am not ashamed of the gospel of Christ: for it is the
power of God unto salvation to every one that believeth;
to the Jew first, and also to the Greek.*

ROMANS 1:16

8

*As ye have therefore received Christ Jesus the Lord,
so walk ye in him: rooted and built up in him,
and stablished in the faith, as ye have been taught,
abounding therein with thanksgiving.*

COLOSSIANS 2:6–7

9

*I am crucified with Christ: nevertheless I live; yet not I,
but Christ liveth in me: and the life which I now live
in the flesh I live by the faith of the Son of God,
who loved me, and gave himself for me.*

GALATIANS 2:20

10

*Only take heed to thyself, and keep thy soul diligently,
lest thou forget the things which thine eyes have seen,
and lest they depart from thy heart all the days of thy life:
but teach them thy sons, and thy sons' sons; specially the
day that thou stoodest before the LORD thy God in Horeb,
when the LORD said unto me, Gather me the people together,
and I will make them hear my words, that they may learn
to fear me all the days that they shall live upon the
earth, and that they may teach their children.*

DEUTERONOMY 4:9–10

11

*But the meek shall inherit the earth; and shall delight
themselves in the abundance of peace.*

PSALM 37:11

12

*I acknowledge my sin unto thee, and mine iniquity have I
not hid. I said, I will confess my transgressions unto
the LORD; and thou forgavest the iniquity of my sin.*

PSALM 32:5

13

*But whoso hearkeneth unto me shall dwell safely,
and shall be quiet from fear of evil.*

PROVERBS 1:33

14

For I am the LORD, I change not;
therefore ye sons of Jacob are not consumed.
MALACHI 3:6

15

The LORD God is my strength, and he will make my feet like
hinds' feet, and he will make me to walk upon mine high
places. To the chief singer on my stringed instruments.
HABAKKUK 3:19

16

If then God so clothe the grass, which is to day in the field,
and to morrow is cast into the oven; how much more
will he clothe you, O ye of little faith?
LUKE 12:28

17

And will be a Father unto you, and ye shall be my sons
and daughters, saith the Lord Almighty.
2 CORINTHIANS 6:18

18

He that descended is the same also that ascended up
far above all heavens, that he might fill all things.
EPHESIANS 4:10

19

Wherefore also it is contained in the scripture, Behold,
I lay in Sion a chief corner stone, elect, precious:
and he that believeth on him shall not be confounded.
1 Peter 2:6

20

For the Lord taketh pleasure in his people:
he will beautify the meek with salvation.
Psalm 149:4

21

The soul of the sluggard desireth, and hath nothing:
but the soul of the diligent shall be made fat.
Proverbs 13:4

22

And, behold, I am with thee, and will keep thee in all
places whither thou goest, and will bring thee again into
this land; for I will not leave thee, until I have
done that which I have spoken to thee of.
Genesis 28:15

23

In whom we have redemption through his blood,
the forgiveness of sins, according to the riches of his grace.
Ephesians 1:7

24

If my people, which are called by my name, shall humble themselves, and pray, and seek my face, and turn from their wicked ways; then will I hear from heaven, and will forgive their sin, and will heal their land.

2 CHRONICLES 7:14

25

In the way of righteousness is life: and in the pathway thereof there is no death.

PROVERBS 12:28

26

Remembering mine affliction and my misery, the wormwood and the gall. . . . This I recall to my mind, therefore have I hope. It is of the LORD's mercies that we are not consumed, because his compassions fail not.

LAMENTATIONS 3:19, 21–22

27

And I will bring the third part through the fire, and will refine them as silver is refined, and will try them as gold is tried: they shall call on my name, and I will hear them: I will say, It is my people: and they shall say, The LORD is my God.

ZECHARIAH 13:9

28

For God so loved the world, that he gave his only begotten
Son, that whosoever believeth in him should not
perish, but have everlasting life.

JOHN 3:16

29

For the promise is unto you, and to your children, and to all
that are afar off, even as many as the LORD our God shall call.

ACTS 2:39

30

Whom I have sent unto you for the same purpose,
that he might know your estate, and comfort your hearts.

COLOSSIANS 4:8

31

The LORD is longsuffering, and of great mercy, forgiving
iniquity and transgression, and by no means clearing
the guilty, visiting the iniquity of the fathers upon
the children unto the third and fourth generation.

NUMBERS 14:18

32

There shall not any man be able to stand before thee all the
days of thy life: as I was with Moses, so I will be with
thee: I will not fail thee, nor forsake thee.

JOSHUA 1:5

33

But when we are judged, we are chastened of the Lord,
that we should not be condemned with the world.
1 CORINTHIANS 11:32

34

By this I know that thou favourest me, because mine enemy
doth not triumph over me. And as for me, thou upholdest me
in mine integrity, and settest me before thy face for ever.
PSALM 41:11–12

35

The LORD thy God in the midst of thee is mighty;
he will save, he will rejoice over thee with joy; he will rest
in his love, he will joy over thee with singing.
ZEPHANIAH 3:17

36

And ye shall be betrayed both by parents, and brethren,
and kinsfolks, and friends; and some of you shall they cause
to be put to death. And ye shall be hated of all men for
my name's sake. But there shall not an hair of your
head perish. In your patience possess ye your souls.
LUKE 21:16–19

37

He hath shewed thee, O man, what is good; and what doth
the LORD require of thee, but to do justly, and to love
mercy, and to walk humbly with thy God?
MICAH 6:8

38

For the hope which is laid up for you in heaven, whereof ye
heard before in the word of the truth of the gospel.
COLOSSIANS 1:5

39

He that hath an ear, let him hear what the Spirit
saith unto the churches; He that overcometh
shall not be hurt of the second death.
REVELATION 2:11

40

Whosoever transgresseth, and abideth not in the doctrine of
Christ, hath not God. He that abideth in the doctrine
of Christ, he hath both the Father and the Son.
2 JOHN 1:9

41

And thou shalt shew thy son in that day, saying,
This is done because of that which the LORD did
unto me when I came forth out of Egypt.
EXODUS 13:8

42

I sought the LORD, and he heard me,
and delivered me from all my fears.

PSALM 34:4

43

Honour the LORD with thy substance, and with the firstfruits
of all thine increase: so shall thy barns be filled with plenty,
and thy presses shall burst out with new wine.

PROVERBS 3:9–10

44

Unto the upright there ariseth light in the darkness:
he is gracious, and full of compassion, and righteous.

PSALM 112:4

45

Humble yourselves therefore under the mighty hand
of God, that he may exalt you in due time.

1 PETER 5:6

46

Return unto thy rest, O my soul; for the LORD
hath dealt bountifully with thee.

PSALM 116:7

47

And saying, The time is fulfilled, and the kingdom of
God is at hand: repent ye, and believe the gospel.

MARK 1:15

48

*Not that we are sufficient of ourselves to think any thing
as of ourselves; but our sufficiency is of God.*

2 CORINTHIANS 3:5

49

*I press toward the mark for the prize of the
high calling of God in Christ Jesus.*

PHILIPPIANS 3:14

50

*How that they told you there should be mockers in the
last time, who should walk after their own ungodly lusts.
These be they who separate themselves, sensual, having not
the Spirit. But ye, beloved, building up yourselves on your
most holy faith, praying in the Holy Ghost, keep yourselves
in the love of God, looking for the mercy of our
Lord Jesus Christ unto eternal life.*

JUDE 18–21

51

*This book of the law shall not depart out of thy mouth;
but thou shalt meditate therein day and night, that thou
mayest observe to do according to all that is written
therein: for then thou shalt make thy way prosperous,
and then thou shalt have good success.*

JOSHUA 1:8

52

*For I was ashamed to require of the king a band of soldiers
and horsemen to help us against the enemy in the way:
because we had spoken unto the king, saying, The hand of
our God is upon all them for good that seek him; but his
power and his wrath is against all them that forsake him.*

EZRA 8:22

53

*Know therefore that the LORD thy God, he is God,
the faithful God, which keepeth covenant and
mercy with them that love him and keep his
commandments to a thousand generations.*

DEUTERONOMY 7:9

54

*Blessed is the man that walketh not in the counsel of the
ungodly, nor standeth in the way of sinners, nor sitteth in
the seat of the scornful. But his delight is in the law of the
LORD; and in his law doth he meditate day and night.*

PSALM 1:1–2

55

*I acknowledge my sin unto thee, and mine iniquity have
I not hid. I said, I will confess my transgressions unto
the LORD; and thou forgavest the iniquity of my sin.*

PSALM 32:5

56

O Lord, thou art my God; I will exalt thee, I will praise thy name; for thou hast done wonderful things; thy counsels of old are faithfulness and truth.

ISAIAH 25:1

57

He will regard the prayer of the destitute, and not despise their prayer.

PSALM 102:17

58

If it be so, our God whom we serve is able to deliver us from the burning fiery furnace, and he will deliver us out of thine hand, O king.

DANIEL 3:17

59

The LORD openeth the eyes of the blind: the LORD raiseth them that are bowed down: the LORD loveth the righteous.

PSALM 146:8

60

Heaviness in the heart of man maketh it stoop: but a good word maketh it glad.

PROVERBS 12:25

61

For he shall give his angels charge over thee, to keep thee in all thy ways. They shall bear thee up in their hands, lest thou dash thy foot against a stone.

PSALM 91:11–12

62

Blessed are they that keep judgment, and he that doeth righteousness at all times.

PSALM 106:3

63

And I will sow her unto me in the earth; and I will have mercy upon her that had not obtained mercy; and I will say to them which were not my people, Thou art my people; and they shall say, Thou art my God.

HOSEA 2:23

64

For there is nothing hid, which shall not be manifested; neither was any thing kept secret, but that it should come abroad.

MARK 4:22

65

For the kingdom of God is not in word, but in power.

1 CORINTHIANS 4:20

66

*For the Lord himself shall descend from heaven with a shout,
with the voice of the archangel, and with the trump of God:
and the dead in Christ shall rise first: then we which
are alive and remain shall be caught up together with
them in the clouds, to meet the Lord in the air: and so shall
we ever be with the Lord. Wherefore comfort
one another with these words.*

1 Thessalonians 4:16–18

67

*Blessed is the man that endureth temptation: for when he
is tried, he shall receive the crown of life, which the
Lord hath promised to them that love him.*

James 1:12

68

*For when God made promise to Abraham, because he could
swear by no greater, he sware by himself, saying, Surely
blessing I will bless thee, and multiplying I will multiply
thee. And so, after he had patiently endured,
he obtained the promise.*

Hebrews 6:13–15

69

*Then he said unto them, Go your way, eat the fat, and drink
the sweet, and send portions unto them for whom nothing is
prepared: for this day is holy unto our LORD: neither be
ye sorry; for the joy of the LORD is your strength.*
NEHEMIAH 8:10

70

*Many are the afflictions of the righteous:
but the LORD delivereth him out of them all.*
PSALM 34:19

71

*Blessed are the poor in spirit:
for theirs is the kingdom of heaven.*
MATTHEW 5:3

72

*That the trial of your faith, being much more precious
than of gold that perisheth, though it be tried with fire,
might be found unto praise and honour and
glory at the appearing of Jesus Christ.*
1 PETER 1:7

73

*And the LORD passed by before him, and proclaimed,
The LORD, The LORD God, merciful and gracious,
longsuffering, and abundant in goodness and truth.*
EXODUS 34:6

74

*I am sought of them that asked not for me; I am found
of them that sought me not: I said, Behold me, behold me.*
ISAIAH 65:1

75

*Thy congregation hath dwelt therein: thou, O God,
hast prepared of thy goodness for the poor.*
PSALM 68:10

76

*For the vision is yet for an appointed time, but at the end
it shall speak, and not lie: though it tarry, wait for it;
because it will surely come, it will not tarry.*
HABAKKUK 2:3

77

*Draw nigh to God, and he will draw nigh to you.
Cleanse your hands, ye sinners; and purify your
hearts, ye double minded.*
JAMES 4:8

78

*My little children, these things write I unto you, that ye sin
not. And if any man sin, we have an advocate with
the Father, Jesus Christ the righteous: and he is the
propitiation for our sins: and not for ours only,
but also for the sins of the whole world.*
1 JOHN 2:1–2

79

*And the L*ORD *said unto him, Peace be unto thee;*
fear not: thou shalt not die.
JUDGES 6:23

80

And thou shalt be secure, because there is hope; yea,
thou shalt dig about thee, and thou shalt take thy rest
in safety. Also thou shalt lie down, and none shall make
thee afraid; yea, many shall make suit unto thee.
JOB 11:18–19

81

For God is my King of old,
working salvation in the midst of the earth.
PSALM 74:12

82

Also unto thee, O Lord, belongeth mercy:
for thou renderest to every man according to his work.
PSALM 62:12

83

Whosoever abideth in him sinneth not:
whosoever sinneth hath not seen him, neither known him.
1 JOHN 3:6

84

And he that overcometh, and keepeth my works unto the end,
to him will I give power over the nations.
REVELATION 2:26

85

The LORD is my strength and song, and he is become
my salvation: he is my God, and I will prepare him
an habitation; my father's God, and I will exalt him.
EXODUS 15:2

86

For thus saith the LORD unto the house of Israel,
Seek ye me, and ye shall live.
AMOS 5:4

87

I will bear the indignation of the LORD, because I have
sinned against him, until he plead my cause, and execute
judgment for me: he will bring me forth to the light,
and I shall behold his righteousness.
MICAH 7:9

88

Mine eyes fail for thy salvation,
and for the word of thy righteousness.
PSALM 119:123

89

Thus saith the LORD, Stand ye in the ways, and see,
and ask for the old paths, where is the good way,
and walk therein, and ye shall find rest for your souls.
But they said, We will not walk therein.
JEREMIAH 6:16

90

Fools make a mock at sin:
but among the righteous there is favour.
PROVERBS 14:9

91

In the multitude of my thoughts
within me thy comforts delight my soul.
PSALM 94:19

92

A new heart also will I give you, and a new spirit will I
put within you: and I will take away the stony heart out
of your flesh, and I will give you an heart of flesh.
EZEKIEL 36:26

93

Therefore I say unto you, Take no thought for your life,
what ye shall eat, or what ye shall drink; nor yet for your
body, what ye shall put on. Is not the life more
than meat, and the body than raiment?
MATTHEW 6:25

94

For the word of God is quick, and powerful, and sharper than any twoedged sword, piercing even to the dividing asunder of soul and spirit, and of the joints and marrow, and is a discerner of the thoughts and intents of the heart.
HEBREWS 4:12

95

Then when lust hath conceived, it bringeth forth sin: and sin, when it is finished, bringeth forth death.
JAMES 1:15

96

It is vain for you to rise up early, to sit up late, to eat the bread of sorrows: for so he giveth his beloved sleep.
PSALM 127:2

97

And whosoever shall exalt himself shall be abased; and he that shall humble himself shall be exalted.
MATTHEW 23:12

98

Also regard not your stuff; for the good of all the land of Egypt is your's.
GENESIS 45:20

99

He shall deliver thee in six troubles:
yea, in seven there shall no evil touch thee.
JOB 5:19

100

He will fulfil the desire of them that fear him:
he also will hear their cry, and will save them.
PSALM 145:19

101

To him give all the prophets witness, that through his name
whosoever believeth in him shall receive remission of sins.
ACTS 10:43

102

And Jesus said unto them, I am the bread of life:
he that cometh to me shall never hunger; and he that
believeth on me shall never thirst.
JOHN 6:35

103

If the Son therefore shall make you free,
ye shall be free indeed.
JOHN 8:36

104

*Therefore being justified by faith, we have peace
with God through our Lord Jesus Christ.*
ROMANS 5:1

105

*And I say unto you, Ask, and it shall be given you;
seek, and ye shall find; knock, and it shall be opened unto you.*
LUKE 11:9

106

*Say ye to the righteous, that it shall be well with him:
for they shall eat the fruit of their doings.*
ISAIAH 3:10

107

*And he shall be like a tree planted by the rivers of water,
that bringeth forth his fruit in his season; his leaf also
shall not wither; and whatsoever he doeth shall prosper.
The ungodly are not so: but are like the chaff
which the wind driveth away.*
PSALM 1:3–4

108

*But I am poor and needy; yet the Lord thinketh
upon me: thou art my help and my deliverer;
make no tarrying, O my God.*
PSALM 40:17

109

Return, ye backsliding children, and I will heal
your backslidings. Behold, we come unto thee;
for thou art the LORD our God.

JEREMIAH 3:22

110

The LORD is good, a strong hold in the day of trouble;
and he knoweth them that trust in him.

NAHUM 1:7

111

Because thou hast kept the word of my patience, I also will
keep thee from the hour of temptation, which shall come
upon all the world, to try them that dwell upon the
earth. Behold, I come quickly: hold that fast
which thou hast, that no man take thy crown.

REVELATION 3:10–11

112

And the work of righteousness shall be peace; and the effect
of righteousness quietness and assurance for ever.

ISAIAH 32:17

113

Thou hast turned for me my mourning into dancing:
thou hast put off my sackcloth, and girded me with gladness.

PSALM 30:11

114

*To set up on high those that be low; that those which
mourn may be exalted to safety.*
JOB 5:11

115

*For whosoever shall do the will of my Father which is in
heaven, the same is my brother, and sister, and mother.*
MATTHEW 12:50

116

But he giveth more grace.
JAMES 4:6

117

*For if these things be in you, and abound, they make you
that ye shall neither be barren nor unfruitful
in the knowledge of our Lord Jesus Christ.*
2 PETER 1:8

118

*I will instruct thee and teach thee in the way which
thou shalt go: I will guide thee with mine eye.*
PSALM 32:8

119

For whosoever will save his life shall lose it;
but whosoever shall lose his life for my sake and
the gospel's, the same shall save it.

MARK 8:35

120

And hope maketh not ashamed; because the love of God
is shed abroad in our hearts by the Holy
Ghost which is given unto us.

ROMANS 5:5

121

Be not deceived; God is not mocked:
for whatsoever a man soweth, that shall he also reap.

GALATIANS 6:7

122

There hath no temptation taken you but such as is common
to man: but God is faithful, who will not suffer you to be
tempted above that ye are able; but will with the temptation
also make a way to escape, that ye may be able to bear it.

1 CORINTHIANS 10:13

123

I will both lay me down in peace, and sleep: for thou,
LORD, only makest me dwell in safety.

PSALM 4:8

124

The wicked is driven away in his wickedness:
but the righteous hath hope in his death.
PROVERBS 14:32

125

And the LORD said unto Moses, Is the LORD's hand waxed
short? thou shalt see now whether my word
shall come to pass unto thee or not.
NUMBERS 11:23

126

Be patient therefore, brethren, unto the coming of the Lord.
Behold, the husbandman waiteth for the precious fruit of
the earth, and hath long patience for it, until he receive the
early and latter rain. Be ye also patient; stablish your
hearts: for the coming of the Lord draweth nigh.
JAMES 5:7–8

127

Beloved, if our heart condemn us not,
then have we confidence toward God.
1 JOHN 3:21

128

But godliness with contentment is great gain.
1 TIMOTHY 6:6

129

*But after that the kindness and love of God our Saviour
toward man appeared, not by works of righteousness
which we have done, but according to his mercy
he saved us, by the washing of regeneration,
and renewing of the Holy Ghost.*

TITUS 3:4–5

130

*And being made perfect, he became the author of eternal
salvation unto all them that obey him.*

HEBREWS 5:9

131

*The Lord knoweth how to deliver the godly out of
temptations, and to reserve the unjust unto the
day of judgment to be punished.*

2 PETER 2:9

132

*But love ye your enemies, and do good, and lend,
hoping for nothing again; and your reward shall be great,
and ye shall be the children of the Highest: for he is
kind unto the unthankful and to the evil.*

LUKE 6:35

133

*Verily, verily, I say unto you, He that heareth my word,
and believeth on him that sent me, hath everlasting life,
and shall not come into condemnation;
but is passed from death unto life.*
JOHN 5:24

134

*Then Jesus beholding him loved him, and said unto him,
One thing thou lackest: go thy way, sell whatsoever thou
hast, and give to the poor, and thou shalt have treasure in
heaven: and come, take up the cross, and follow me.*
MARK 10:21

135

*For God giveth to a man that is good in his sight wisdom,
and knowledge, and joy: but to the sinner he giveth travail,
to gather and to heap up, that he may give to him that is
good before God. This also is vanity and vexation of spirit.*
ECCLESIASTES 2:26

136

*And therefore will the LORD wait, that he may be gracious
unto you, and therefore will he be exalted, that he may have
mercy upon you: for the LORD is a God of judgment:
blessed are all they that wait for him.*
ISAIAH 30:18

137

Sing unto the LORD, praise ye the LORD: for he hath delivered the soul of the poor from the hand of evildoers.
JEREMIAH 20:13

138

Be merciful unto me, O God, be merciful unto me: for my soul trusteth in thee: yea, in the shadow of thy wings will I make my refuge, until these calamities be overpast.
PSALM 57:1

139

Be thou my strong habitation, whereunto I may continually resort: thou hast given commandment to save me; for thou art my rock and my fortress.
PSALM 71:3

140

Although my house be not so with God; yet he hath made with me an everlasting covenant, ordered in all things, and sure: for this is all my salvation, and all my desire, although he make it not to grow.
2 SAMUEL 23:5

141

But the hour cometh, and now is, when the true worshippers shall worship the Father in spirit and in truth: for the Father seeketh such to worship him.
JOHN 4:23

142

*Repent ye therefore, and be converted, that your sins
may be blotted out, when the times of refreshing
shall come from the presence of the Lord.*
ACTS 3:19

143

*Blessed is every one that feareth the LORD;
that walketh in his ways.*
PSALM 128:1

144

*Thou shalt be hid from the scourge of the tongue:
neither shalt thou be afraid of destruction when it cometh.*
JOB 5:21

145

*The LORD is good unto them that wait for him,
to the soul that seeketh him.*
LAMENTATIONS 3:25

146

*Bring ye all the tithes into the storehouse, that there may
be meat in mine house, and prove me now herewith,
saith the LORD of hosts, if I will not open you the
windows of heaven, and pour you out a blessing,
that there shall not be room enough to receive it.*
MALACHI 3:10

147

For thou, Lord, art good, and ready to forgive;
and plenteous in mercy unto all them that call upon thee.
PSALM 86:5

148

And they shall no more be a prey to the heathen,
neither shall the beast of the land devour them; but they shall
dwell safely, and none shall make them afraid.
EZEKIEL 34:28

149

I have shewed you all things, how that so labouring ye ought
to support the weak, and to remember the words of the Lord
Jesus, how he said, It is more blessed to give than to receive.
ACTS 20:35

150

He that loveth his brother abideth in the light,
and there is none occasion of stumbling in him.
1 JOHN 2:10

151

But continue thou in the things which thou hast learned
and hast been assured of, knowing of whom
thou hast learned them.
2 TIMOTHY 3:14

152

*That being justified by his grace, we should be made
heirs according to the hope of eternal life.*
TITUS 3:7

153

*The LORD is gracious, and full of compassion;
slow to anger, and of great mercy.*
PSALM 145:8

154

*Fear thou not; for I am with thee: be not dismayed; for I am
thy God: I will strengthen thee; yea, I will help thee; yea,
I will uphold thee with the right hand of my righteousness.*
ISAIAH 41:10

155

*Like as a father pitieth his children,
so the LORD pitieth them that fear him.*
PSALM 103:13

156

*That we should be saved from our enemies, and from the
hand of all that hate us; to perform the mercy promised
to our fathers, and to remember his holy covenant.*
LUKE 1:71–72

157

For thou, LORD, wilt bless the righteous;
with favour wilt thou compass him as with a shield.
PSALM 5:12

158

For if, when we were enemies, we were reconciled to
God by the death of his Son, much more, being reconciled,
we shall be saved by his life. And not only so,
but we also joy in God through our Lord Jesus Christ,
by whom we have now received the atonement.
ROMANS 5:10–11

159

He shall redeem their soul from deceit and violence:
and precious shall their blood be in his sight.
PSALM 72:14

160

Through God we shall do valiantly: for he it is
that shall tread down our enemies.
PSALM 60:12

161

Nevertheless he left not himself without witness,
in that he did good, and gave us rain from heaven,
and fruitful seasons, filling our hearts with food and gladness.
ACTS 14:17

162

*Take heed therefore how ye hear: for whosoever hath, to him shall
be given; and whosoever hath not, from him shall be
taken even that which he seemeth to have.*

LUKE 8:18

163

*Therefore it is of faith, that it might be by grace; to the end
the promise might be sure to all the seed; not to that only
which is of the law, but to that also which is of the
faith of Abraham; who is the father of us all.*

ROMANS 4:16

164

*Blessed be God, even the Father of our Lord Jesus Christ,
the Father of mercies, and the God of all comfort; who comforteth
us in all our tribulation, that we may be able to comfort
them which are in any trouble, by the comfort
wherewith we ourselves are comforted of God.*

2 CORINTHIANS 1:3–4

165

*Wherefore, my beloved, as ye have always obeyed,
not as in my presence only, but now much more in my
absence, work out your own salvation with fear and
trembling. For it is God which worketh in you
both to will and to do of his good pleasure.*

PHILIPPIANS 2:12–13

166

And ye shall serve the LORD your God, and he shall
bless thy bread, and thy water; and I will take
sickness away from the midst of thee.
EXODUS 23:25

167

If thou wouldest seek unto God betimes, and make thy
supplication to the Almighty; if thou wert pure and
upright; surely now he would awake for thee, and make the
habitation of thy righteousness prosperous.
JOB 8:5–6

168

The LORD is righteous in all his ways,
and holy in all his works.
PSALM 145:17

169

The LORD is merciful and gracious,
slow to anger, and plenteous in mercy.
PSALM 103:8

170

Behold, it is written before me: I will not keep silence,
but will recompense, even recompense into their bosom.
ISAIAH 65:6

171

Light is sown for the righteous, and gladness for the upright
in heart. Rejoice in the LORD, ye righteous; and give thanks
at the remembrance of his holiness.
PSALM 97:11–12

172

And many of them that sleep in the dust of the earth
shall awake, some to everlasting life, and some
to shame and everlasting contempt.
DANIEL 12:2

173

No man hath seen God at any time. If we love one
another, God dwelleth in us, and his love is perfected in us.
1 JOHN 4:12

174

For the which cause I also suffer these things:
nevertheless I am not ashamed: for I know whom
I have believed, and am persuaded that he is able to
keep that which I have committed unto him against that day.
2 TIMOTHY 1:12

175

But the wisdom that is from above is first pure, then
peaceable, gentle, and easy to be intreated, full of mercy
and good fruits, without partiality, and without hypocrisy.
JAMES 3:17

176

He will swallow up death in victory; and the Lord GOD
will wipe away tears from off all faces; and the rebuke
of his people shall he take away from off all the
earth: for the LORD hath spoken it.
ISAIAH 25:8

177

The righteousness of the perfect shall direct his way:
but the wicked shall fall by his own wickedness.
PROVERBS 11:5

178

Nevertheless we, according to his promise, look for new
heavens and a new earth, wherein dwelleth righteousness.
2 PETER 3:13

179

Then shall we know, if we follow on to know the LORD:
his going forth is prepared as the morning; and he shall come
unto us as the rain, as the latter and former rain unto the earth.
HOSEA 6:3

180

Then shall he give the rain of thy seed, that thou shalt
sow the ground withal; and bread of the increase
of the earth, and it shall be fat and plenteous:
in that day shall thy cattle feed in large pastures.
ISAIAH 30:23

181

And, lo, I am with you always, even unto the end of the world.
MATTHEW 28:20

182

*For the people shall dwell in Zion at Jerusalem: thou shalt
weep no more: he will be very gracious unto thee at the voice
of thy cry; when he shall hear it, he will answer thee.*
ISAIAH 30:19

183

*Lo, children are an heritage of the LORD: and the fruit of the
womb is his reward. As arrows are in the hand of a mighty
man; so are children of the youth. Happy is the man that
hath his quiver full of them: they shall not be ashamed,
but they shall speak with the enemies in the gate.*
PSALM 127:3–5

184

*But as many as received him, to them gave he power to become
the sons of God, even to them that believe on his name.*
JOHN 1:12

185

*And he said unto Jesus, Lord, remember me when thou
comest into thy kingdom. And Jesus said unto him,
Verily I say unto thee, Today shalt thou
be with me in paradise.*
LUKE 23:42–43

186

And he said, My presence shall go with thee,
and I will give thee rest.
EXODUS 33:14

187

For if ye turn again unto the LORD, your brethren and
your children shall find compassion before them that lead
them captive, so that they shall come again into this land:
for the LORD your God is gracious and merciful, and will not
turn away his face from you, if ye return unto him.
2 CHRONICLES 30:9

188

For his anger endureth but a moment; in his favour
is life: weeping may endure for a night,
but joy cometh in the morning.
PSALM 30:5

189

Turn you at my reproof: behold, I will pour out my spirit
unto you, I will make known my words unto you.
PROVERBS 1:23

190

If ye then, being evil, know how to give good gifts unto your
children, how much more shall your Father which
is in heaven give good things to them that ask him?
MATTHEW 7:11

191

Heaven and earth shall pass away,
but my words shall not pass away.
MATTHEW 24:35

192

He staggered not at the promise of God through unbelief;
but was strong in faith, giving glory to God; and being
fully persuaded that, what he had promised,
he was able also to perform.
ROMANS 4:20–21

193

Who being the brightness of his glory, and the express
image of his person, and upholding all things by the word
of his power, when he had by himself purged our sins,
sat down on the right hand of the Majesty on high.
HEBREWS 1:3

194

Thou tellest my wanderings: put thou my tears into thy bottle:
are they not in thy book? When I cry unto thee, then shall
mine enemies turn back: this I know; for God is for me.
In God will I praise his word: in the LORD will I praise
his word. In God have I put my trust: I will not
be afraid what man can do unto me.
PSALM 56:8–11

195

Trust ye in the LORD for ever: for in the LORD
JEHOVAH is everlasting strength.
ISAIAH 26:4

196

Heal me, O LORD, and I shall be healed; save me,
and I shall be saved: for thou art my praise.
JEREMIAH 17:14

197

And the Spirit and the bride say, Come. And let him that
heareth say, Come. And let him that is athirst come. And
whosoever will, let him take the water of life freely.
REVELATION 22:17

198

A wise man will hear, and will increase learning;
and a man of understanding shall attain unto wise counsels.
PROVERBS 1:5

199

Blessed is the man whom thou chastenest, O LORD,
and teachest him out of thy law; that thou mayest
give him rest from the days of adversity,
until the pit be digged for the wicked.
PSALM 94:12–13

200

But thou, O LORD, art a shield for me;
my glory, and the lifter up of mine head.
PSALM 3:3

201

For all those things hath mine hand made, and all those
things have been, saith the LORD: but to this man
will I look, even to him that is poor and of a
contrite spirit, and trembleth at my word.
ISAIAH 66:2

202

Lay not up for yourselves treasures upon earth, where moth
and rust doth corrupt, and where thieves break through
and steal: but lay up for yourselves treasures in heaven,
where neither moth nor rust doth corrupt, and where
thieves do not break through nor steal: for where
your treasure is, there will your heart be also.
MATTHEW 6:19–21

203

But we are bound to give thanks alway to God for you,
brethren beloved of the Lord, because God hath from
the beginning chosen you to salvation through
sanctification of the Spirit and belief of the truth.
2 THESSALONIANS 2:13

204

In hope of eternal life, which God, that cannot lie,
promised before the world began.
TITUS 1:2

205

But with righteousness shall he judge the poor, and reprove
with equity for the meek of the earth: and he shall smite
the earth: with the rod of his mouth, and with the
breath of his lips shall he slay the wicked.
ISAIAH 11:4

206

Blessed are they that mourn: for they shall be comforted.
MATTHEW 5:4

207

And rend your heart, and not your garments, and turn unto
the LORD your God: for he is gracious and merciful, slow to
anger, and of great kindness, and repenteth him of the evil.
JOEL 2:13

208

So when this corruptible shall have put on incorruption,
and this mortal shall have put on immortality, then shall
be brought to pass the saying that is written, Death is
swallowed up in victory. O death, where is thy
sting? O grave, where is thy victory?
1 CORINTHIANS 15:54–55

209

Yea, before the day was I am he; and there is none that can deliver out of my hand: I will work, and who shall let it?
ISAIAH 43:13

210

O love the LORD, all ye his saints: for the LORD preserveth the faithful, and plentifully rewardeth the proud doer.
PSALM 31:23

211

God is jealous, and the LORD revengeth; the LORD revengeth, and is furious; the LORD will take vengeance on his adversaries, and he reserveth wrath for his enemies.
NAHUM 1:2

212

Whosoever therefore shall humble himself as this little child, the same is greatest in the kingdom of heaven.
MATTHEW 18:4

213

But, beloved, be not ignorant of this one thing, that one day is with the Lord as a thousand years, and a thousand years as one day. The Lord is not slack concerning his promise, as some men count slackness; but is longsuffering to us-ward, not willing that any should perish, but that all should come to repentance.
2 PETER 3:8–9

214

And the world passeth away, and the lust thereof:
but he that doeth the will of God abideth for ever.
1 JOHN 2:17

215

For the LORD will not cast off for ever: but though he
cause grief, yet will he have compassion according to
the multitude of his mercies. For he doth not afflict
willingly nor grieve the children of men.
LAMENTATIONS 3:31–33

216

Hath walked in my statutes, and hath kept
my judgments, to deal truly; he is just,
he shall surely live, saith the Lord GOD.
EZEKIEL 18:9

217

And the LORD, he it is that doth go before thee;
he will be with thee, he will not fail thee,
neither forsake thee: fear not, neither be dismayed.
DEUTERONOMY 31:8

218

Seek good, and not evil, that ye may live: and so the LORD,
the God of hosts, shall be with you, as ye have spoken.
AMOS 5:14

219

*Think not that I am come to destroy the law, or the prophets:
I am not come to destroy, but to fulfil. For verily I say unto
you, Till heaven and earth pass, one jot or one tittle shall
in no wise pass from the law, till all be fulfilled.*

MATTHEW 5:17–18

220

*For the mountains shall depart, and the hills be removed;
but my kindness shall not depart from thee, neither shall
the covenant of my peace be removed,
saith the LORD that hath mercy on thee.*

ISAIAH 54:10

221

*But one in a certain place testified, saying, What is man,
that thou art mindful of him? or the son of man that thou
visitest him? Thou madest him a little lower than the angels;
thou crownedst him with glory and honour, and didst set
him over the works of thy hands: thou hast put all things in
subjection under his feet. For in that he put all in subjection
under him, he left nothing that is not put under him.
But now we see not yet all things put under him.*

HEBREWS 2:6–8

222

*As for man, his days are as grass: as a flower of the field,
so he flourisheth. For the wind passeth over it, and it is
gone; and the place thereof shall know it no more.
But the mercy of the LORD is from everlasting
to everlasting upon them that fear him,
and his righteousness unto children's children.*

PSALM 103:15–17

223

*Let no man say when he is tempted, I am tempted
of God: for God cannot be tempted with evil,
neither tempteth he any man.*

JAMES 1:13

224

*Be ye therefore merciful, as your Father also is merciful.
Judge not, and ye shall not be judged: condemn not,
and ye shall not be condemned: forgive,
and ye shall be forgiven.*

LUKE 6:36–37

225

*And it shall come to pass in the day that the LORD shall
give thee rest from thy sorrow, and from thy fear,
and from the hard bondage wherein thou
wast made to serve.*

ISAIAH 14:3

226

*Yea, if thou criest after knowledge, and liftest up thy voice
for understanding; if thou seekest her as silver, and searchest
for her as for hid treasures; then shalt thou understand the
fear of the LORD, and find the knowledge of God.*

PROVERBS 2:3–5

227

*For to be carnally minded is death; but to be spiritually
minded is life and peace.*

ROMANS 8:6

228

*For we are his workmanship, created in Christ Jesus
unto good works, which God hath before
ordained that we should walk in them.*

EPHESIANS 2:10

229

*For the scripture saith,
Whosoever believeth on him shall not be ashamed.*

ROMANS 10:11

230

*For thou shalt eat the labour of thine hands:
happy shalt thou be, and it shall be well with thee.*

PSALM 128:2

231

So shall they fear the name of the LORD from the west,
and his glory from the rising of the sun. When the enemy
shall come in like a flood, the Spirit of the LORD
shall lift up a standard against him.

ISAIAH 59:19

232

But he that doeth truth cometh to the light, that his deeds
may be made manifest, that they are wrought in God.

JOHN 3:21

233

As it is written, Behold, I lay in Sion a stumblingstone
and rock of offence: and whosoever believeth
on him shall not be ashamed.

ROMANS 9:33

234

Being confident of this very thing, that he which hath
begun a good work in you will perform it
until the day of Jesus Christ.

PHILIPPIANS 1:6

235

I create the fruit of the lips; Peace, peace to him that is far off,
and to him that is near, saith the LORD; and I will heal him.

ISAIAH 57:19

236

The LORD also will be a refuge for the oppressed,
a refuge in times of trouble.
PSALM 9:9

237

Thou, which hast shewed me great and sore troubles,
shalt quicken me again, and shalt bring me up again
from the depths of the earth. Thou shalt increase
my greatness, and comfort me on every side.
PSALM 71:20–21

238

Now if the fall of them be the riches of the world,
and the diminishing of them the riches of the Gentiles;
how much more their fulness?
ROMANS 11:12

239

So that ye come behind in no gift;
waiting for the coming of our Lord Jesus Christ.
1 CORINTHIANS 1:7

240

For in him dwelleth all the fulness of the Godhead bodily.
And ye are complete in him, which is the head
of all principality and power.
COLOSSIANS 2:9–10

241

The lip of truth shall be established for ever:
but a lying tongue is but for a moment.
PROVERBS 12:19

242

Let the wicked forsake his way, and the unrighteous
man his thoughts: and let him return unto the LORD,
and he will have mercy upon him; and to our
God, for he will abundantly pardon.
ISAIAH 55:7

243

For ye have need of patience, that, after ye have
done the will of God, ye might receive the promise.
HEBREWS 10:36

244

The words of a man's mouth are as deep waters,
and the wellspring of wisdom as a flowing brook.
PROVERBS 18:4

245

For I will restore health unto thee, and I will heal thee of
thy wounds, saith the LORD; because they called thee an
Outcast, saying, This is Zion, whom no man seeketh after.
JEREMIAH 30:17

246

And fear not them which kill the body, but are not able
to kill the soul: but rather fear him which is
able to destroy both soul and body in hell.
MATTHEW 10:28

247

And they said, Believe on the Lord Jesus Christ,
and thou shalt be saved, and thy house.
ACTS 16:31

248

Who delivered us from so great a death, and doth deliver:
in whom we trust that he will yet deliver us.
2 CORINTHIANS 1:10

249

That if thou shalt confess with thy mouth the Lord Jesus,
and shalt believe in thine heart that God hath raised
him from the dead, thou shalt be saved.
ROMANS 10:9

250

With long life will I satisfy him, and shew him my salvation.
PSALM 91:16

251

Ye that love the LORD, hate evil: he preserveth the souls of his saints; he delivereth them out of the hand of the wicked.
PSALM 97:10

252

And she shall bring forth a son, and thou shalt call his name JESUS: for he shall save his people from their sins.
MATTHEW 1:21

253

I say unto you, that likewise joy shall be in heaven over one sinner that repenteth, more than over ninety and nine just persons, which need no repentance.
LUKE 15:7

254

For in that he himself hath suffered being tempted, he is able to succour them that are tempted.
HEBREWS 2:18

255

My brethren, count it all joy when ye fall into divers temptations; knowing this, that the trying of your faith worketh patience. But let patience have her perfect work, that ye may be perfect and entire, wanting nothing.
JAMES 1:2–4

256

But if we walk in the light, as he is in the light,
we have fellowship one with another, and the blood
of Jesus Christ his Son cleanseth us from all sin.
1 John 1:7

257

And he said, I will make all my goodness pass before thee,
and I will proclaim the name of the LORD before thee;
and will be gracious to whom I will be gracious,
and will shew mercy on whom I will shew mercy.
Exodus 33:19

258

But he saveth the poor from the sword, from their mouth,
and from the hand of the mighty. So the poor hath hope,
and iniquity stoppeth her mouth.
Job 5:15–16

259

When his disciples heard it, they were exceedingly amazed,
saying, Who then can be saved? But Jesus beheld them,
and said unto them, With men this is impossible;
but with God all things are possible.
Matthew 19:25–26

260

Behold, God is my salvation; I will trust, and not be afraid:
for the Lord Jehovah is my strength and my song;
he also is become my salvation.
Isaiah 12:2

261

They that trust in the Lord shall be as mount Zion,
which cannot be removed, but abideth for ever.
Psalm 125:1

262

Come, and let us return unto the Lord: for he hath torn,
and he will heal us; he hath smitten, and he will bind us up.
Hosea 6:1

263

Likewise the Spirit also helpeth our infirmities: for we know
not what we should pray for as we ought: but the Spirit
itself maketh intercession for us with
groanings which cannot be uttered.
Romans 8:26

264

Having predestinated us unto the adoption of children
by Jesus Christ to himself, according to the
good pleasure of his will.
Ephesians 1:5

265

For whatsoever things were written aforetime were
written for our learning, that we through patience and
comfort of the scriptures might have hope.

ROMANS 15:4

266

This then is the message which we have heard of him,
and declare unto you, that God is light,
and in him is no darkness at all.

1 JOHN 1:5

267

Fear not; for thou shalt not be ashamed: neither be thou
confounded; for thou shalt not be put to shame: for thou shalt
forget the shame of thy youth, and shalt not remember
the reproach of thy widowhood any more.

ISAIAH 54:4

268

Hope deferred maketh the heart sick:
but when the desire cometh, it is a tree of life.

PROVERBS 13:12

269

*Behold, I shew you a mystery; We shall not all sleep, but we
shall all be changed, in a moment, in the twinkling of an eye,
at the last trump: for the trumpet shall sound, and the dead
shall be raised incorruptible, and we shall be changed.
For this corruptible must put on incorruption,
and this mortal must put on immortality.*
1 CORINTHIANS 15:51–53

270

*The LORD will give strength unto his people;
the LORD will bless his people with peace.*
PSALM 29:11

271

*For God hath not given us the spirit of fear;
but of power, and of love, and of a sound mind.*
2 TIMOTHY 1:7

272

*For we are made partakers of Christ, if we hold the
beginning of our confidence stedfast unto the end.*
HEBREWS 3:14

273

Let the brother of low degree rejoice in that he is exalted.
JAMES 1:9

274

And above all things have fervent charity among yourselves:
for charity shall cover the multitude of sins.

1 PETER 4:8

275

And we know that all things work together for good
to them that love God, to them who are
the called according to his purpose.

ROMANS 8:28

276

The way of the just is uprightness: thou, most upright, dost
weigh the path of the just. Yea, in the way of thy judgments,
O LORD, have we waited for thee; the desire of our soul
is to thy name, and to the remembrance of thee.

ISAIAH 26:7–8

277

The LORD is my strength and my shield; my heart trusted
in him, and I am helped: therefore my heart greatly
rejoiceth; and with my song will I praise him.

PSALM 28:7

278

*Are there any among the vanities of the Gentiles that can
cause rain? or can the heavens give showers? art not thou
he, O LORD our God? therefore we will wait upon
thee: for thou hast made all these things.*

JEREMIAH 14:22

279

*Therefore whosoever heareth these sayings of mine, and doeth
them, I will liken him unto a wise man, which built his house
upon a rock: and the rain descended, and the floods came,
and the winds blew, and beat upon that house;
and it fell not: for it was founded upon a rock.*

MATTHEW 7:24–25

280

*Because the foolishness of God is wiser than men;
and the weakness of God is stronger than men.*

1 CORINTHIANS 1:25

281

*In whom ye also trusted, after that ye heard the word of
truth, the gospel of your salvation: in whom also after that
ye believed, ye were sealed with that holy Spirit of promise,
which is the earnest of our inheritance until the redemption
of the purchased possession, unto the praise of his glory.*

EPHESIANS 1:13–14

282

Behold, what manner of love the Father hath bestowed upon us, that we should be called the sons of God: therefore the world knoweth us not, because it knew him not.

1 JOHN 3:1

283

For ye have not received the spirit of bondage again to fear; but ye have received the Spirit of adoption, whereby we cry, Abba, Father.

ROMANS 8:15

284

Therefore if any man be in Christ, he is a new creature: old things are passed away; behold, all things are become new.

2 CORINTHIANS 5:17

285

Thou art my hiding place; thou shalt preserve me from trouble; thou shalt compass me about with songs of deliverance.

PSALM 32:7

286

God setteth the solitary in families: he bringeth out those which are bound with chains: but the rebellious dwell in a dry land.

PSALM 68:6

287

At destruction and famine thou shalt laugh:
neither shalt thou be afraid of the beasts of the earth.
JOB 5:22

288

Blessed be the LORD, that hath given rest unto his people
Israel, according to all that he promised: there hath not failed
one word of all his good promise, which he promised
by the hand of Moses his servant.
1 KINGS 8:56

289

Rejoice not against me, O mine enemy: when I fall,
I shall arise; when I sit in darkness,
the LORD shall be a light unto me.
MICAH 7:8

290

Wealth gotten by vanity shall be diminished:
but he that gathereth by labour shall increase.
PROVERBS 13:11

291

Incline your ear, and come unto me: hear, and your soul
shall live; and I will make an everlasting covenant
with you, even the sure mercies of David.
ISAIAH 55:3

292

As the living Father hath sent me, and I live by the Father:
so he that eateth me, even he shall live by me.
JOHN 6:57

293

But if the Spirit of him that raised up Jesus from the dead
dwell in you, he that raised up Christ from the dead shall
also quicken your mortal bodies by his Spirit
that dwelleth in you.
ROMANS 8:11

294

The light of the body is the eye: if therefore thine eye
be single, thy whole body shall be full of light.
MATTHEW 6:22

295

For the LORD giveth wisdom: out of his mouth cometh
knowledge and understanding. He layeth up sound wisdom
for the righteous: he is a buckler to them that walk uprightly.
PROVERBS 2:6–7

296

If in this life only we have hope in Christ, we are of all men
most miserable. But now is Christ risen from the dead,
and become the firstfruits of them that slept.
1 CORINTHIANS 15:19–20

297

And he said unto me, It is done. I am Alpha and Omega,
the beginning and the end. I will give unto him that
is athirst of the fountain of the water of life freely.
REVELATION 21:6

298

But he was wounded for our transgressions, he was bruised
for our iniquities: the chastisement of our peace was
upon him; and with his stripes we are healed.
ISAIAH 53:5

299

Fear not: for I am with thee: I will bring thy seed from the
east, and gather thee from the west; I will say to the north,
Give up; and to the south, Keep not back: bring my sons from
far, and my daughters from the ends of the earth; even every
one that is called by my name: for I have created him for
my glory, I have formed him; yea, I have made him.
ISAIAH 43:5–7

300

For God, who commanded the light to shine out of darkness,
hath shined in our hearts, to give the light of the knowledge
of the glory of God in the face of Jesus Christ.
2 CORINTHIANS 4:6

301

For they that are after the flesh do mind the things of the flesh; but they that are after the Spirit the things of the Spirit.
ROMANS 8:5

302

Be careful for nothing; but in every thing by prayer and supplication with thanksgiving let your requests be made known unto God.
PHILIPPIANS 4:6

303

But is now made manifest by the appearing of our Saviour Jesus Christ, who hath abolished death, and hath brought life and immortality to light through the gospel.
2 TIMOTHY 1:10

304

And this is the promise that he hath promised us, even eternal life.
1 JOHN 2:25

305

Now faith is the substance of things hoped for, the evidence of things not seen.
HEBREWS 11:1

306

For, behold, I create new heavens and a new earth:
and the former shall not be remembered, nor come into mind.
ISAIAH 65:17

307

O give thanks unto the LORD, for he is good:
for his mercy endureth for ever.
PSALM 107:1

308

Whom resist stedfast in the faith, knowing that the same
afflictions are accomplished in your brethren that are in the
world. But the God of all grace, who hath called us unto his
eternal glory by Christ Jesus, after that ye have suffered a
while, make you perfect, stablish, strengthen, settle you.
1 PETER 5:9–10

309

But I have trusted in thy mercy;
my heart shall rejoice in thy salvation.
PSALM 13:5

310

Commit thy works unto the LORD,
and thy thoughts shall be established.
PROVERBS 16:3

311

But unto you that fear my name shall the Sun of righteousness
arise with healing in his wings; and ye shall go forth,
and grow up as calves of the stall.

MALACHI 4:2

312

In that he saith, A new covenant, he hath made
the first old. Now that which decayeth and
waxeth old is ready to vanish away.

HEBREWS 8:13

313

And Jesus answered and said unto her, Martha, Martha,
thou art careful and troubled about many things:
but one thing is needful: and Mary hath chosen that
good part, which shall not be taken away from her.

LUKE 10:41–42

314

For by grace are ye saved through faith;
and that not of yourselves: it is the gift of God.

EPHESIANS 2:8

315

For as many as are led by the Spirit of God,
they are the sons of God.

ROMANS 8:14

316

By faith the walls of Jericho fell down,
after they were compassed about seven days.
HEBREWS 11:30

317

He giveth power to the faint; and to them
that have no might he increaseth strength.
ISAIAH 40:29

318

Let not thine heart envy sinners: but be thou in the fear
of the LORD all the day long. For surely there is an end;
and thine expectation shall not be cut off.
PROVERBS 23:17–18

319

So also is the resurrection of the dead. It is sown in
corruption; it is raised in incorruption: it is sown
in dishonour; it is raised in glory: it is sown
in weakness; it is raised in power.
1 CORINTHIANS 15:42–43

320

The highway of the upright is to depart from evil:
he that keepeth his way preserveth his soul.
PROVERBS 16:17

321

Behold, they shall surely gather together, but not by me:
whosoever shall gather together against
thee shall fall for thy sake.
ISAIAH 54:15

322

O give thanks unto the LORD; for he is good: for his mercy
endureth for ever. O give thanks unto the God of gods:
for his mercy endureth for ever. O give thanks to
the Lord of lords: for his mercy endureth for ever.
PSALM 136:1–3

323

And I will give them one heart, and I will put a new spirit
within you; and I will take the stony heart out of their flesh,
and will give them an heart of flesh: that they may walk
in my statutes, and keep mine ordinances, and do them:
and they shall be my people, and I will be their God.
EZEKIEL 11:19–20

324

Therefore take no thought, saying, What shall we eat?
or, What shall we drink? or, Wherewithal shall we be
clothed? (For after all these things do the Gentiles seek:)
for your heavenly Father knoweth that ye
have need of all these things.
MATTHEW 6:31–32

325

*For which cause we faint not; but though our outward
man perish, yet the inward man is renewed day by day.
For our light affliction, which is but for a moment,
worketh for us a far more exceeding
and eternal weight of glory.*

2 CORINTHIANS 4:16–17

326

*Those things, which ye have both learned,
and received, and heard, and seen in me, do:
and the God of peace shall be with you.*

PHILIPPIANS 4:9

327

*My sheep hear my voice, and I know them, and they follow
me: and I give unto them eternal life; and they shall never
perish, neither shall any man pluck them out of my hand.*

JOHN 10:27–28

328

*Dearly beloved, avenge not yourselves,
but rather give place unto wrath: for it is written,
Vengeance is mine; I will repay, saith the Lord.*

ROMANS 12:19

329

*And ye now therefore have sorrow: but I will see
you again, and your heart shall rejoice,
and your joy no man taketh from you.*
JOHN 16:22

330

*And they shall teach no more every man his neighbour,
and every man his brother, saying, Know the LORD:
for they shall all know me, from the least of them unto the
greatest of them, saith the LORD: for I will forgive their
iniquity, and I will remember their sin no more.*
JEREMIAH 31:34

331

*And all thy children shall be taught of the LORD;
and great shall be the peace of thy children.*
ISAIAH 54:13

332

*The LORD shall preserve thy going out and thy coming
in from this time forth, and even for evermore.*
PSALM 121:8

333

*When a wicked man dieth, his expectation shall perish:
and the hope of unjust men perisheth. The righteous
is delivered out of trouble.*
PROVERBS 11:7–8

334

Many sorrows shall be to the wicked: but he that
trusteth in the LORD, mercy shall compass him about.
PSALM 32:10

335

But he that shall endure unto the end,
the same shall be saved.
MATTHEW 24:13

336

Much more then, being now justified by his blood,
we shall be saved from wrath through him.
ROMANS 5:9

337

And now abideth faith, hope, charity,
these three; but the greatest of these is charity.
1 CORINTHIANS 13:13

338

But without faith it is impossible to please him: for he that
cometh to God must believe that he is, and that he is
a rewarder of them that diligently seek him.
HEBREWS 11:6

339

And every man that hath this hope in him
purifieth himself, even as he is pure.

1 John 3:3

340

And when they bring you unto the synagogues, and unto
magistrates, and powers, take ye no thought how or what
thing ye shall answer, or what ye shall say: for the Holy Ghost
shall teach you in the same hour what ye ought to say.

Luke 12:11–12

341

He loveth righteousness and judgment:
the earth is full of the goodness of the Lord.

Psalm 33:5

342

All the earth shall worship thee,
and shall sing unto thee; they shall sing to thy name.

Psalm 66:4

343

Hear therefore, O Israel, and observe to do it; that it
may be well with thee, and that ye may increase mightily,
as the Lord God of thy fathers hath promised thee,
in the land that floweth with milk and honey.

Deuteronomy 6:3

344

Be ye strong therefore, and let not your hands
be weak: for your work shall be rewarded.
2 CHRONICLES 15:7

345

The eternal God is thy refuge, and underneath are
the everlasting arms: and he shall thrust out the enemy
from before thee; and shall say, Destroy them.
DEUTERONOMY 33:27

346

Thou shalt come to thy grave in a full age,
like as a shock of corn cometh in in his season.
JOB 5:26

347

The fear of the LORD is the beginning of wisdom:
and the knowledge of the holy is understanding.
PROVERBS 9:10

348

Thou art wearied in the greatness of thy way; yet saidst thou
not, There is no hope: thou hast found the life of thine
hand; therefore thou wast not grieved.
ISAIAH 57:10

349

Verily, verily, I say unto you,
He that believeth on me hath everlasting life.
JOHN 6:47

350

And we desire that every one of you do shew the
same diligence to the full assurance of hope unto the end:
that ye be not slothful, but followers of them who
through faith and patience inherit the promises.
HEBREWS 6:11–12

351

Whose adorning let it not be that outward adorning of
plaiting the hair, and of wearing of gold, or of putting on
of apparel; but let it be the hidden man of the heart, in that
which is not corruptible, even the ornament of a meek and
quiet spirit, which is in the sight of God of great price.
1 PETER 3:3–4

352

And who is he that will harm you,
if ye be followers of that which is good?
1 PETER 3:13

353

Behold, the Lord GOD *will come with strong hand,
and his arm shall rule for him: behold, his reward is
with him, and his work before him. He shall feed his
flock like a shepherd: he shall gather the lambs
with his arm, and carry them in his bosom,
and shall gently lead those that are with young.*

ISAIAH 40:10–11

354

*Search the scriptures; for in them ye think ye have
eternal life: and they are they which testify of me.*

JOHN 5:39

355

The LORD *is good to all:
and his tender mercies are over all his works.*

PSALM 145:9

356

*For the rod of the wicked shall not rest upon the lot
of the righteous; lest the righteous put forth
their hands unto iniquity.*

PSALM 125:3

357

*Take heed that ye do not your alms before men, to be seen of
them: otherwise ye have no reward of your Father which is
in heaven. Therefore when thou doest thine alms, do not
sound a trumpet before thee, as the hypocrites do in the
synagogues and in the streets, that they may have glory
of men. Verily I say unto you, They have their reward.
But when thou doest alms, let not thy left hand
know what thy right hand doeth: that thine
alms may be in secret: and thy Father which
seeth in secret himself shall reward thee openly.*
MATTHEW 6:1–4

358

*Behold, the LORD's hand is not shortened,
that it cannot save; neither his ear heavy, that it cannot hear.*
ISAIAH 59:1

359

*In righteousness shalt thou be established: thou shalt be
far from oppression; for thou shalt not fear:
and from terror; for it shall not come near thee.*
ISAIAH 54:14

360

*The glory of young men is their strength:
and the beauty of old men is the grey head.*
PROVERBS 20:29

361

He that covereth his sins shall not prosper:
but whoso confesseth and forsaketh them shall have mercy.
PROVERBS 28:13

362

God is our refuge and strength, a very present help in trouble.
Therefore will not we fear, though the earth be removed,
and though the mountains be carried into the midst of the
sea; though the waters thereof roar and be troubled,
though the mountains shake with the swelling thereof.
PSALM 46:1–3

363

Then shall ye call upon me, and ye shall go
and pray unto me, and I will hearken unto you.
JEREMIAH 29:12

364

But go ye and learn what that meaneth, I will have
mercy, and not sacrifice: for I am not come to call
the righteous, but sinners to repentance.
MATTHEW 9:13

365

For I am with thee, and no man shall set on thee
to hurt thee: for I have much people in this city.
ACTS 18:10

366

*Therefore I say unto you, What things soever ye desire,
when ye pray, believe that ye receive
them, and ye shall have them.*

MARK 11:24

367

*Be not ye therefore like unto them: for your Father knoweth
what things ye have need of, before ye ask him.*

MATTHEW 6:8

368

*For the creature was made subject to vanity, not willingly,
but by reason of him who hath subjected the same in hope,
because the creature itself also shall be delivered
from the bondage of corruption into the
glorious liberty of the children of God.*

ROMANS 8:20–21

369

*For all the promises of God in him are yea,
and in him Amen, unto the glory of God by us.*

2 CORINTHIANS 1:20

370

*Let us hold fast the profession of our faith
without wavering; (for he is faithful that promised).*

HEBREWS 10:23

371

*Marvel not at this: for the hour is coming, in the which
all that are in the graves shall hear his voice,
and shall come forth; they that have done good, unto the
resurrection of life; and they that have done evil,
unto the resurrection of damnation.*

JOHN 5:28–29

372

*Not every one that saith unto me, Lord, Lord,
shall enter into the kingdom of heaven; but he that
doeth the will of my Father which is in heaven.*

MATTHEW 7:21

373

*The king's heart is in the hand of the LORD,
as the rivers of water: he turneth it whithersoever he will.*

PROVERBS 21:1

374

*Herein is my Father glorified, that ye bear much fruit;
so shall ye be my disciples.*

JOHN 15:8

375

*Jesus saith unto him, Thomas, because thou hast seen me,
thou hast believed: blessed are they that have
not seen, and yet have believed.*

JOHN 20:29

376

And I have declared unto them thy name,
and will declare it: that the love wherewith thou
hast loved me may be in them, and I in them.
JOHN 17:26

377

Thou wilt keep him in perfect peace,
whose mind is stayed on thee: because he trusteth in thee.
ISAIAH 26:3

378

A false balance is abomination to the LORD:
but a just weight is his delight.
PROVERBS 11:1

379

And not only so, but we glory in tribulations also:
knowing that tribulation worketh patience.
ROMANS 5:3

380

I will abundantly bless her provision:
I will satisfy her poor with bread.
PSALM 132:15

381

*Therefore I take pleasure in infirmities, in reproaches,
in necessities, in persecutions, in distresses for Christ's
sake: for when I am weak, then am I strong.*
2 CORINTHIANS 12:10

382

*That Christ may dwell in your hearts by faith; that ye,
being rooted and grounded in love, may be able to
comprehend with all saints what is the breadth,
and length, and depth, and height; and to know
the love of Christ, which passeth knowledge,
that ye might be filled with all the fulness of God.*
EPHESIANS 3:17–19

383

*But I would not have you to be ignorant, brethren,
concerning them which are asleep, that ye sorrow not,
even as others which have no hope. For if we believe
that Jesus died and rose again, even so them also
which sleep in Jesus will God bring with him.*
1 THESSALONIANS 4:13–14

384

Jesus Christ the same yesterday, and to day, and for ever.
HEBREWS 13:8

385

*Henceforth I call you not servants; for the servant knoweth
not what his lord doeth: but I have called you friends;
for all things that I have heard of my Father
I have made known unto you.*

JOHN 15:15

386

*Sell that ye have, and give alms; provide yourselves bags
which wax not old, a treasure in the heavens that faileth
not, where no thief approacheth, neither moth corrupteth.*

LUKE 12:33

387

*And kings shall be thy nursing fathers, and their queens thy
nursing mothers: they shall bow down to thee with their
face toward the earth, and lick up the dust of thy feet;
and thou shalt know that I am the LORD:
for they shall not be ashamed that wait for me.*

ISAIAH 49:23

388

*Better is a dry morsel, and quietness therewith,
than an house full of sacrifices with strife.*

PROVERBS 17:1

389

*Wait on the LORD: be of good courage, and he shall
strengthen thine heart: wait, I say, on the LORD.*
PSALM 27:14

390

*But seek ye first the kingdom of God, and his righteousness;
and all these things shall be added unto you.*
MATTHEW 6:33

391

*Verily, verily, I say unto you, That ye shall weep and lament,
but the world shall rejoice: and ye shall be sorrowful,
but your sorrow shall be turned into joy.*
JOHN 16:20

392

*Give, and it shall be given unto you; good measure,
pressed down, and shaken together, and running over,
shall men give into your bosom. For with the same measure
that ye mete withal it shall be measured to you again.*
LUKE 6:38

393

Watch ye, stand fast in the faith, quit you like men, be strong.
1 CORINTHIANS 16:13

394

He that goeth forth and weepeth, bearing precious seed,
shall doubtless come again with rejoicing,
bringing his sheaves with him.

PSALM 126:6

395

Thy righteousness is like the great mountains;
thy judgments are a great deep: O LORD,
thou preservest man and beast.

PSALM 36:6

396

But if from thence thou shalt seek the LORD thy God,
thou shalt find him, if thou seek him with
all thy heart and with all thy soul.

DEUTERONOMY 4:29

397

If iniquity be in thine hand, put it far away, and let not
wickedness dwell in thy tabernacles. For then shalt thou
lift up thy face without spot; yea, thou shalt be
stedfast, and shalt not fear.

JOB 11:14–15

398

And all things, whatsoever ye shall ask in prayer,
believing, ye shall receive.

MATTHEW 21:22

399

The LORD upholdeth all that fall,
and raiseth up all those that be bowed down.
PSALM 145:14

400

Therefore the redeemed of the LORD shall return,
and come with singing unto Zion; and everlasting joy
shall be upon their head: they shall obtain gladness
and joy; and sorrow and mourning shall flee away.
ISAIAH 51:11

401

Ye have not chosen me, but I have chosen you, and ordained
you, that ye should go and bring forth fruit, and that your
fruit should remain: that whatsoever ye shall ask of
the Father in my name, he may give it you.
JOHN 15:16

402

Evening, and morning, and at noon, will I pray,
and cry aloud: and he shall hear my voice.
PSALM 55:17

403

But it is good for me to draw near to God: I have put my
trust in the Lord GOD, that I may declare all thy works.
PSALM 73:28

404

And ye shall seek me, and find me,
when ye shall search for me with all your heart.
Jeremiah 29:13

405

Jesus said unto him, If thou wilt be perfect, go and sell that
thou hast, and give to the poor, and thou shalt have
treasure in heaven: and come and follow me.
Matthew 19:21

406

The Spirit itself beareth witness with our spirit, that we are
the children of God: and if children, then heirs; heirs of God,
and joint-heirs with Christ; if so be that we suffer
with him, that we may be also glorified together.
Romans 8:16–17

407

Yea doubtless, and I count all things but loss for the excellency
of the knowledge of Christ Jesus my Lord: for whom I
have suffered the loss of all things, and do count
them but dung, that I may win Christ.
Philippians 3:8

408

*But the natural man receiveth not the things of the Spirit
of God: for they are foolishness unto him: neither can
he know them, because they are spiritually discerned.
But he that is spiritual judgeth all things,
yet he himself is judged of no man.*
1 CORINTHIANS 2:14–15

409

*Cast not away therefore your confidence,
which hath great recompence of reward.*
HEBREWS 10:35

410

*And now, little children, abide in him; that,
when he shall appear, we may have confidence,
and not be ashamed before him at his coming.*
1 JOHN 2:28

411

*All we like sheep have gone astray; we have turned
every one to his own way; and the LORD hath
laid on him the iniquity of us all.*
ISAIAH 53:6

412

*Blessed is the man that trusteth in the L*ORD*, and whose hope the L*ORD *is. For he shall be as a tree planted by the waters, and that spreadeth out her roots by the river, and shall not see when heat cometh, but her leaf shall be green; and shall not be careful in the year of drought, neither shall cease from yielding fruit.*
JEREMIAH 17:7–8

413

All the days of the afflicted are evil: but he that is of a merry heart hath a continual feast.
PROVERBS 15:15

414

He that believeth on him is not condemned: but he that believeth not is condemned already, because he hath not believed in the name of the only begotten Son of God.
JOHN 3:18

415

As many as I love, I rebuke and chasten: be zealous therefore, and repent.
REVELATION 3:19

416

Through faith also Sara herself received strength to conceive seed, and was delivered of a child when she was past age, because she judged him faithful who had promised.
HEBREWS 11:11

417

But whosoever drinketh of the water that I shall give him shall never thirst; but the water that I shall give him shall be in him a well of water springing up into everlasting life.
JOHN 4:14

418

Sow to yourselves in righteousness, reap in mercy; break up your fallow ground: for it is time to seek the LORD, till he come and rain righteousness upon you.
HOSEA 10:12

419

The name of the LORD is a strong tower: the righteous runneth into it, and is safe.
PROVERBS 18:10

420

Ointment and perfume rejoice the heart: so doth the sweetness of a man's friend by hearty counsel.
PROVERBS 27:9

421

And to love him with all the heart, and with all the
understanding, and with all the soul, and with all
the strength, and to love his neighbour as himself,
is more than all whole burnt offerings and sacrifices.
MARK 12:33

422

He that keepeth the commandment keepeth his own soul;
but he that despiseth his ways shall die.
PROVERBS 19:16

423

Bless the LORD, O my soul, and forget not all his benefits:
who forgiveth all thine iniquities; who healeth all thy
diseases; who redeemeth thy life from destruction;
who crowneth thee with lovingkindness and tender mercies.
PSALM 103:2–4

424

No weapon that is formed against thee shall prosper;
and every tongue that shall rise against thee in judgment
thou shalt condemn. This is the heritage of the servants of
the LORD, and their righteousness is of me, saith the LORD.
ISAIAH 54:17

425

In the day when I cried thou answeredst me,
and strengthenedst me with strength in my soul.

PSALM 138:3

426

Now therefore ye are no more strangers and foreigners,
but fellowcitizens with the saints,
and of the household of God.

EPHESIANS 2:19

427

But God hath chosen the foolish things of the world to
confound the wise; and God hath chosen the weak things
of the world to confound the things which are mighty;
and base things of the world, and things which are despised,
hath God chosen, yea, and things which are not, to bring to
nought things that are: that no flesh should glory in
his presence. But of him are ye in Christ Jesus,
who of God is made unto us wisdom,
and righteousness, and sanctification,
and redemption.

1 CORINTHIANS 1:27–30

428

*Therefore, brethren, we are debtors, not to the flesh,
to live after the flesh. For if ye live after the flesh,
ye shall die: but if ye through the Spirit do
mortify the deeds of the body, ye shall live.*

ROMANS 8:12–13

429

*So that we may boldly say, The Lord is my helper,
and I will not fear what man shall do unto me.*

HEBREWS 13:6

430

*Praise ye the LORD. Blessed is the man that feareth the
LORD, that delighteth greatly in his commandments. . . .
Wealth and riches shall be in his house:
and his righteousness endureth for ever.*

PSALM 112:1, 3

431

*Only fear the LORD, and serve him in truth with all your
heart: for consider how great things he hath done for you.*

1 SAMUEL 12:24

432

Remember ye not the former things, neither consider the things of old. Behold, I will do a new thing; now it shall spring forth; shall ye not know it? I will even make a way in the wilderness, and rivers in the desert.

Isaiah 43:18–19

433

The angel of the LORD encampeth round about them that fear him, and delivereth them.

Psalm 34:7

434

For thou art my hope, O Lord GOD: thou art my trust from my youth.

Psalm 71:5

435

A little that a righteous man hath is better than the riches of many wicked.

Psalm 37:16

436

As far as the east is from the west, so far hath he removed our transgressions from us.

Psalm 103:12

437

Blessed are they which do hunger and thirst after
righteousness: for they shall be filled.
MATTHEW 5:6

438

The hope of the righteous shall be gladness:
but the expectation of the wicked shall perish.
PROVERBS 10:28

439

That they should seek the Lord, if haply they might feel after
him, and find him, though he be not far from every one of us.
ACTS 17:27

440

Who against hope believed in hope, that he might
become the father of many nations, according to
that which was spoken, So shall thy seed be.
ROMANS 4:18

441

My soul, wait thou only upon God;
for my expectation is from him.
PSALM 62:5

442

For ye shall go out with joy, and be led forth with peace:
the mountains and the hills shall break forth before you into
singing, and all the trees of the field shall clap their hands.

ISAIAH 55:12

443

God is not a man, that he should lie; neither the son of man,
that he should repent: hath he said, and shall he not do it?
or hath he spoken, and shall he not make it good?

NUMBERS 23:19

444

And it shall come to pass, that before they call, I will answer;
and while they are yet speaking, I will hear.

ISAIAH 65:24

445

Verily, verily, I say unto you, If a man keep my saying,
he shall never see death.

JOHN 8:51

446

Beloved, let us love one another: for love is of God;
and every one that loveth is born of God, and knoweth God.

1 JOHN 4:7

447

*For thus saith the high and lofty One that inhabiteth
eternity, whose name is Holy; I dwell in the high and holy
place, with him also that is of a contrite and humble spirit,
to revive the spirit of the humble, and to revive
the heart of the contrite ones.*

ISAIAH 57:15

448

*The young lions do lack, and suffer hunger: but they that
seek the LORD shall not want any good thing.*

PSALM 34:10

449

*Though ye have lien among the pots, yet shall ye
be as the wings of a dove covered with silver,
and her feathers with yellow gold.*

PSALM 68:13

450

*And of Benjamin he said, The beloved of the LORD shall dwell
in safety by him; and the Lord shall cover him all the day
long, and he shall dwell between his shoulders.*

DEUTERONOMY 33:12

451

*If, when evil cometh upon us, as the sword, judgment,
or pestilence, or famine, we stand before this house,
and in thy presence, (for thy name is in this house,)
and cry unto thee in our affliction,
then thou wilt hear and help.*

2 Chronicles 20:9

452

*The integrity of the upright shall guide them:
but the perverseness of transgressors shall destroy them.*

Proverbs 11:3

453

*(For the LORD thy God is a merciful God;) he will not
forsake thee, neither destroy thee, nor forget the
covenant of thy fathers which he sware unto them.*

Deuteronomy 4:31

454

*And the King shall answer and say unto them,
Verily I say unto you, Inasmuch as ye have done it unto one
of the least of these my brethren, ye have done it unto me.*

Matthew 25:40

455

But go thou thy way till the end be: for thou shalt rest,
and stand in thy lot at the end of the days.
DANIEL 12:13

456

My soul melteth for heaviness:
strengthen thou me according unto thy word.
PSALM 119:28

457

The LORD shall preserve thee from all evil:
he shall preserve thy soul.
PSALM 121:7

458

And he answered, Fear not: for they that be with us
are more than they that be with them.
2 KINGS 6:16

459

And thine age shall be clearer than the noonday:
thou shalt shine forth, thou shalt be as the morning.
JOB 11:17

460

And he will love thee, and bless thee, and multiply thee:
he will also bless the fruit of thy womb, and the fruit of thy
land, thy corn, and thy wine, and thine oil, the increase of
thy kine, and the flocks of thy sheep, in the land which
he sware unto thy fathers to give thee.

DEUTERONOMY 7:13

461

Hearken, my beloved brethren, Hath not God chosen the poor
of this world rich in faith, and heirs of the kingdom
which he hath promised to them that love him?

JAMES 2:5

462

For God is not unrighteous to forget your work and labour
of love, which ye have shewed toward his name, in that ye
have ministered to the saints, and do minister.

HEBREWS 6:10

463

Fret not thyself because of evildoers, neither be thou envious
against the workers of iniquity. For they shall soon be cut
down like the grass, and wither as the green herb.

PSALM 37:1–2

464

Therefore they shall come and sing in the height of Zion,
and shall flow together to the goodness of the LORD,
for wheat, and for wine, and for oil, and for the young of
the flock and of the herd: and their soul shall be as a watered
garden; and they shall not sorrow any more at all.
JEREMIAH 31:12

465

The LORD shall cause thine enemies that rise up against
thee to be smitten before thy face: they shall come out
against thee one way, and flee before thee seven ways.
DEUTERONOMY 28:7

466

And I say also unto thee, That thou art Peter, and upon this
rock I will build my church; and the gates of
hell shall not prevail against it.
MATTHEW 16:18

467

That the blessing of Abraham might come on the Gentiles
through Jesus Christ; that we might receive
the promise of the Spirit through faith.
GALATIANS 3:14

468

*Trust in the LORD with all thine heart; and lean not
unto thine own understanding. In all thy ways
acknowledge him, and he shall direct thy paths.*
PROVERBS 3:5–6

469

*For ye know the grace of our Lord Jesus Christ, that,
though he was rich, yet for your sakes he became
poor, that ye through his poverty might be rich.*
2 CORINTHIANS 8:9

470

*Ye have put off the old man with his deeds; and have put
on the new man, which is renewed in knowledge
after the image of him that created him.*
COLOSSIANS 3:9–10

471

*He hath given meat unto them that fear him:
he will ever be mindful of his covenant.*
PSALM 111:5

472

*To every thing there is a season,
and a time to every purpose under the heaven.*
ECCLESIASTES 3:1

473

But the LORD is my defence;
and my God is the rock of my refuge.
PSALM 94:22

474

Whereby are given unto us exceeding great and precious
promises: that by these ye might be partakers
of the divine nature, having escaped the
corruption that is in the world through lust.
2 PETER 1:4

475

Beloved, think it not strange concerning the fiery trial which
is to try you, as though some strange thing happened unto you:
but rejoice, inasmuch as ye are partakers of Christ's sufferings;
that, when his glory shall be revealed, ye may be
glad also with exceeding joy.
1 PETER 4:12–13

476

Righteousness exalteth a nation:
but sin is a reproach to any people.
PROVERBS 14:34

477

*See, I have set before thee this day life and good, and death
and evil; in that I command thee this day to love the* LORD
*thy God, to walk in his ways, and to keep his commandments
and his statutes and his judgments, that thou mayest live
and multiply: and the* LORD *thy God shall bless thee
in the land whither thou goest to possess it.*

DEUTERONOMY 30:15–16

478

*And he said unto him, Son, thou art ever with me,
and all that I have is thine.*

LUKE 15:31

479

*For as by one man's disobedience many were made sinners,
so by the obedience of one shall many be made righteous.*

ROMANS 5:19

480

*He that trusteth in his riches shall fall;
but the righteous shall flourish as a branch.*

PROVERBS 11:28

481

*But as for me, I will come into thy house in the multitude
of thy mercy: and in thy fear will I worship
toward thy holy temple.*

PSALM 5:7

482

If any man's work shall be burned, he shall suffer loss:
but he himself shall be saved; yet so as by fire.
1 CORINTHIANS 3:15

483

For by one offering he hath perfected
for ever them that are sanctified.
HEBREWS 10:14

484

But ye are a chosen generation, a royal priesthood,
an holy nation, a peculiar people; that ye should shew
forth the praises of him who hath called you out
of darkness into his marvellous light.
1 PETER 2:9

485

And whatsoever we ask, we receive of him,
because we keep his commandments, and do those
things that are pleasing in his sight.
1 JOHN 3:22

486

*Lift up your eyes to the heavens, and look upon the earth
beneath: for the heavens shall vanish away like smoke, and
the earth shall wax old like a garment, and they that dwell
therein shall die in like manner: but my salvation shall be
for ever, and my righteousness shall not be abolished.*

ISAIAH 51:6

487

*Know therefore this day, and consider it in thine heart,
that the LORD he is God in heaven above,
and upon the earth beneath: there is none else.*

DEUTERONOMY 4:39

488

*And also the Strength of Israel will not lie nor repent:
for he is not a man, that he should repent.*

1 SAMUEL 15:29

489

*Yea, I will rejoice over them to do them good, and I will
plant them in this land assuredly with my
whole heart and with my whole soul.*

JEREMIAH 32:41

490

When he maketh inquisition for blood,
he remembereth them: he forgetteth not the cry of the humble.
PSALM 9:12

491

Cast thy burden upon the LORD, and he shall sustain thee:
he shall never suffer the righteous to be moved.
PSALM 55:22

492

My flesh and my heart faileth: but God is the strength
of my heart, and my portion for ever.
PSALM 73:26

493

Confess your faults one to another, and pray one for another,
that ye may be healed. The effectual fervent prayer
of a righteous man availeth much.
JAMES 5:16

494

Casting all your care upon him; for he careth for you.
1 PETER 5:7

495

For we know that if our earthly house of this tabernacle
were dissolved, we have a building of God, an house not
made with hands, eternal in the heavens.

2 Corinthians 5:1

496

Though I walk in the midst of trouble, thou wilt revive me:
thou shalt stretch forth thine hand against the wrath
of mine enemies, and thy right hand shall save me.

Psalm 138:7

497

He found him in a desert land, and in the waste howling
wilderness; he led him about, he instructed him,
he kept him as the apple of his eye.

Deuteronomy 32:10

498

I will ransom them from the power of the grave;
I will redeem them from death: O death, I will be
thy plagues; O grave, I will be thy destruction:
repentance shall be hid from mine eyes.

Hosea 13:14

499

I will not leave you comfortless: I will come to you.

John 14:18

500

As the Father hath loved me, so have I loved you: continue
ye in my love. If ye keep my commandments, ye shall abide
in my love; even as I have kept my Father's commandments,
and abide in his love. These things have I spoken unto
you, that my joy might remain in you,
and that your joy might be full.
JOHN 15:9–11

501

Because he hath set his love upon me,
therefore will I deliver him: I will set him
on high, because he hath known my name.
PSALM 91:14

502

Knowing this, that our old man is crucified with him,
that the body of sin might be destroyed, that henceforth we
should not serve sin. For he that is dead is freed from sin.
ROMANS 6:6–7

503

The eyes of the LORD are in every place,
beholding the evil and the good.
PROVERBS 15:3

504

The humble shall see this, and be glad:
and your heart shall live that seek God.
Psalm 69:32

505

The lines are fallen unto me in pleasant places;
yea, I have a goodly heritage.
Psalm 16:6

506

Nay, in all these things we are more than conquerors
through him that loved us. For I am persuaded, that neither
death, nor life, nor angels, nor principalities, nor powers,
nor things present, nor things to come, nor height, nor depth,
nor any other creature, shall be able to separate us from
the love of God, which is in Christ Jesus our Lord.
Romans 8:37–39

507

Honour thy father and mother; which is the first
commandment with promise; that it may be well
with thee, and thou mayest live long on the earth.
Ephesians 6:2–3

508

Fear not, little flock; for it is your Father's good
pleasure to give you the kingdom.
LUKE 12:32

509

But thus saith the LORD, Even the captives of the mighty
shall be taken away, and the prey of the terrible shall
be delivered: for I will contend with him that
contendeth with thee, and I will save thy children.
ISAIAH 49:25

510

The fear of the wicked, it shall come upon him:
but the desire of the righteous shall be granted.
PROVERBS 10:24

511

But my God shall supply all your need according
to his riches in glory by Christ Jesus.
PHILIPPIANS 4:19

512

For as in Adam all die,
even so in Christ shall all be made alive.
1 CORINTHIANS 15:22

513

For if our heart condemn us,
God is greater than our heart, and knoweth all things.
1 John 3:20

514

The steps of a good man are ordered by the Lord:
and he delighteth in his way.
Psalm 37:23

515

Be strong and of a good courage, fear not, nor be afraid
of them: for the Lord thy God, he it is that doth
go with thee; he will not fail thee, nor forsake thee.
Deuteronomy 31:6

516

He shall not be afraid of evil tidings:
his heart is fixed, trusting in the Lord.
Psalm 112:7

517

As a shepherd seeketh out his flock in the day that he is among
his sheep that are scattered; so will I seek out my sheep,
and will deliver them out of all places where they
have been scattered in the cloudy and dark day.
Ezekiel 34:12

518

*Thou hast seen it; for thou beholdest mischief and spite,
to requite it with thy hand: the poor committeth
himself unto thee; thou art the helper of the fatherless.*

PSALM 10:14

519

*So that a man shall say, Verily there is a reward for the
righteous: verily he is a God that judgeth in the earth.*

PSALM 58:11

520

*For I have said, Mercy shall be built up for ever:
thy faithfulness shalt thou establish in the very heavens.*

PSALM 89:2

521

*For if ye forgive men their trespasses,
your heavenly Father will also forgive you.*

MATTHEW 6:14

522

*For the righteous LORD loveth righteousness;
his countenance doth behold the upright.*

PSALM 11:7

523

And he that keepeth his commandments dwelleth in him,
and he in him. And hereby we know that he
abideth in us, by the Spirit which he hath given us.
1 JOHN 3:24

524

As newborn babes, desire the sincere milk of the word,
that ye may grow thereby.
1 PETER 2:2

525

The LORD hath appeared of old unto me, saying, Yea,
I have loved thee with an everlasting love:
therefore with lovingkindness have I drawn thee.
JEREMIAH 31:3

526

Howbeit when he, the Spirit of truth, is come, he will guide
you into all truth: for he shall not speak of himself;
but whatsoever he shall hear, that shall he speak:
and he will shew you things to come.
JOHN 16:13

527

Thou openest thine hand,
and satisfiest the desire of every living thing.
PSALM 145:16

528

*Who hath ascended up into heaven, or descended?
who hath gathered the wind in his fists? who hath
bound the waters in a garment? who hath established
all the ends of the earth? what is his name, and what is
his son's name, if thou canst tell? Every word of God is
pure: he is a shield unto them that put their trust in him.*
PROVERBS 30:4–5

529

*But when thou makest a feast, call the poor,
the maimed, the lame, the blind: and thou shalt be
blessed; for they cannot recompense thee: for thou
shalt be recompensed at the resurrection of the just.*
LUKE 14:13–14

530

*The LORD hath prepared his throne in the heavens;
and his kingdom ruleth over all.*
PSALM 103:19

531

*The blessing of the LORD, it maketh rich,
and he addeth no sorrow with it.*
PROVERBS 10:22

532

His heart is established, he shall not be afraid,
until he see his desire upon his enemies.
PSALM 112:8

533

And now come I to thee; and these things I speak in the
world, that they might have my joy fulfilled in themselves.
JOHN 17:13

534

Know ye not that ye are the temple of God,
and that the Spirit of God dwelleth in you?
1 CORINTHIANS 3:16

535

LORD, thou hast heard the desire of the humble:
thou wilt prepare their heart,
thou wilt cause thine ear to hear.
PSALM 10:17

536

But God will redeem my soul from
the power of the grave: for he shall receive me.
PSALM 49:15

537

Ye shall walk in all the ways which the LORD your God
hath commanded you, that ye may live, and that it
may be well with you, and that ye may prolong
your days in the land which ye shall possess.
DEUTERONOMY 5:33

538

For the LORD heareth the poor,
and despiseth not his prisoners.
PSALM 69:33

539

For the LORD God is a sun and shield: the LORD will
give grace and glory: no good thing will he
withhold from them that walk uprightly.
PSALM 84:11

540

Behold, thou desirest truth in the inward parts:
and in the hidden part thou shalt make me to know wisdom.
PSALM 51:6

541

Behold, he that keepeth Israel shall neither slumber nor sleep.
PSALM 121:4

542

*Therefore now let it please thee to bless the house of thy
servant, that it may continue for ever before thee: for thou,
O Lord GOD, hast spoken it: and with thy blessing
let the house of thy servant be blessed for ever.*

2 SAMUEL 7:29

543

*And though after my skin worms destroy this body,
yet in my flesh shall I see God: whom I shall see for
myself, and mine eyes shall behold, and not another;
though my reins be consumed within me.*

JOB 19:26–27

544

*Let the field be joyful, and all that is therein: then shall
all the trees of the wood rejoice before the LORD: for he cometh,
for he cometh to judge the earth: he shall judge the world
with righteousness, and the people with his truth.*

PSALM 96:12–13

545

*I in them, and thou in me, that they may be made perfect in
one; and that the world may know that thou hast sent me,
and hast loved them, as thou hast loved me.*

JOHN 17:23

546

He healeth the broken in heart,
and bindeth up their wounds.
PSALM 147:3

547

I the LORD have called thee in righteousness, and will hold
thine hand, and will keep thee, and give thee for a covenant
of the people, for a light of the Gentiles; to open the blind eyes,
to bring out the prisoners from the prison, and them that
sit in darkness out of the prison house.
ISAIAH 42:6–7

548

But the righteousness which is of faith speaketh on this
wise, Say not in thine heart, Who shall ascend into heaven?
(that is, to bring Christ down from above:) or,
Who shall descend into the deep? (that is, to bring up
Christ again from the dead.) But what saith it?
The word is nigh thee, even in thy mouth, and in thy
heart: that is, the word of faith, which we preach.
ROMANS 10:6–8

549

For ye are all the children of God by faith in Christ Jesus.
GALATIANS 3:26

550

*How much more shall the blood of Christ, who through the
eternal Spirit offered himself without spot to God,
purge your conscience from dead works
to serve the living God?*

HEBREWS 9:14

551

*The righteous cry, and the LORD heareth,
and delivereth them out of all their troubles.*

PSALM 34:17

552

*Why sayest thou, O Jacob, and speakest, O Israel,
My way is hid from the LORD, and my judgment
is passed over from my God? Hast thou not known?
hast thou not heard, that the everlasting God, the LORD,
the Creator of the ends of the earth, fainteth not,
neither is weary? there is no searching
of his understanding.*

ISAIAH 40:27–28

553

*And it shall be to me a name of joy, a praise and an honour
before all the nations of the earth, which shall hear all the good
that I do unto them: and they shall fear and tremble for all the
goodness and for all the prosperity that I procure unto it.*

JEREMIAH 33:9

554

The labour of the righteous tendeth to life:
the fruit of the wicked to sin.

PROVERBS 10:16

555

Ye that fear the LORD, trust in the LORD:
he is their help and their shield.

PSALM 115:11

556

Because thou shalt forget thy misery,
and remember it as waters that pass away.

JOB 11:16

557

For the needy shall not always be forgotten:
the expectation of the poor shall not perish for ever.

PSALM 9:18

558

And ye shall eat in plenty, and be satisfied, and praise the
name of the LORD your God, that hath dealt wondrously
with you: and my people shall never be ashamed.

JOEL 2:26

559

I have called upon thee, for thou wilt hear me,
O God: incline thine ear unto me, and hear my speech.
PSALM 17:6

560

The law of the LORD is perfect, converting the soul:
the testimony of the LORD is sure, making wise the simple.
PSALM 19:7

561

When my father and my mother forsake me,
then the LORD will take me up.
PSALM 27:10

562

They that dwell under his shadow shall return;
they shall revive as the corn, and grow as the vine:
the scent thereof shall be as the wine of Lebanon.
HOSEA 14:7

563

And I will bring the blind by a way that they knew not;
I will lead them in paths that they have not known:
I will make darkness light before them, and crooked things
straight. These things will I do unto them,
and not forsake them.
ISAIAH 42:16

564

He hath remembered his covenant for ever,
the word which he commanded to a thousand generations.
PSALM 105:8

565

Every good gift and every perfect gift is from above,
and cometh down from the Father of lights, with whom is
no variableness, neither shadow of turning.
JAMES 1:17

566

Yet setteth he the poor on high from affliction,
and maketh him families like a flock.
PSALM 107:41

567

Do they not err that devise evil?
but mercy and truth shall be to them that devise good.
PROVERBS 14:22

568

And, Thou, Lord, in the beginning hast laid the foundation
of the earth; and the heavens are the works of thine hands:
they shall perish; but thou remainest; and they all shall wax
old as doth a garment; and as a vesture shalt thou fold
them up, and they shall be changed: but thou
art the same, and thy years shall not fail.
HEBREWS 1:10–12

569

Blessed be the God and Father of our Lord Jesus Christ,
which according to his abundant mercy hath begotten us
again unto a lively hope by the resurrection of Jesus Christ
from the dead, to an inheritance incorruptible, and undefiled,
and that fadeth not away, reserved in heaven for you,
who are kept by the power of God through faith unto
salvation ready to be revealed in the last time.
1 PETER 1:3–5

570

Wherefore he is able also to save them to the uttermost
that come unto God by him, seeing he ever
liveth to make intercession for them.
HEBREWS 7:25

571

The way of the slothful man is as an hedge of thorns:
but the way of the righteous is made plain.
PROVERBS 15:19

572

Trust in the LORD, and do good; so shalt thou dwell
in the land, and verily thou shalt be fed.
PSALM 37:3

573

For the which cause I also suffer these things:
nevertheless I am not ashamed: for I know whom
I have believed, and am persuaded that he is able
to keep that which I have committed
unto him against that day.
2 TIMOTHY 1:12

574

And we have known and believed the love that God
hath to us. God is love; and he that dwelleth
in love dwelleth in God, and God in him.
1 JOHN 4:16

575

Blessed is he that readeth, and they that hear the words
of this prophecy, and keep those things which are
written therein: for the time is at hand.
REVELATION 1:3

576

My soul shall be satisfied as with marrow and fatness;
and my mouth shall praise thee with joyful lips.
PSALM 63:5

577

The righteous shall be glad in the LORD, and shall trust
in him; and all the upright in heart shall glory.
PSALM 64:10

578

*Wherefore it shall come to pass, if ye hearken to these
judgments, and keep, and do them, that the LORD
thy God shall keep unto thee the covenant and
the mercy which he sware unto thy fathers.*

DEUTERONOMY 7:12

579

*And have hope toward God, which they themselves
also allow, that there shall be a resurrection
of the dead, both of the just and unjust.*

ACTS 24:15

580

*Also now, behold, my witness is in heaven,
and my record is on high.*

JOB 16:19

581

*Nevertheless I am continually with thee: thou hast holden me
by my right hand. Thou shalt guide me with thy counsel,
and afterward receive me to glory.*

PSALM 73:23–24

582

*For this God is our God for ever and ever:
he will be our guide even unto death.*

PSALM 48:14

583

For as the sufferings of Christ abound in us,
so our consolation also aboundeth by Christ.
2 CORINTHIANS 1:5

584

Delight thyself also in the LORD:
and he shall give thee the desires of thine heart.
PSALM 37:4

585

Neither is there any creature that is not manifest
in his sight: but all things are naked and opened
unto the eyes of him with whom we have to do.
HEBREWS 4:13

586

Thou wilt shew me the path of life: in thy presence is fulness
of joy; at thy right hand there are pleasures for evermore.
PSALM 16:11

587

Thou shalt surely give him, and thine heart shall not be
grieved when thou givest unto him: because that for this
thing the LORD thy God shall bless thee in all thy works,
and in all that thou puttest thine hand unto.
DEUTERONOMY 15:10

588

*Take therefore no thought for the morrow: for the
morrow shall take thought for the things of itself.
Sufficient unto the day is the evil thereof.*
MATTHEW 6:34

589

*Moreover the law entered, that the offence might abound.
But where sin abounded, grace did much more abound:
that as sin hath reigned unto death, even so might
grace reign through righteousness unto
eternal life by Jesus Christ our Lord.*
ROMANS 5:20–21

590

*The LORD trieth the righteous: but the wicked
and him that loveth violence his soul hateth.*
PSALM 11:5

591

*And I will cleanse them from all their iniquity,
whereby they have sinned against me; and I will pardon
all their iniquities, whereby they have sinned,
and whereby they have transgressed against me.*
JEREMIAH 33:8

592

*I am the good shepherd, and know my sheep, and am known
of mine. As the Father knoweth me, even so know I
the Father: and I lay down my life for the sheep. And other
sheep I have, which are not of this fold: them also
I must bring, and they shall hear my voice;
and there shall be one fold, and one shepherd.*
JOHN 10:14–16

593

*For sin shall not have dominion over you:
for ye are not under the law, but under grace.*
ROMANS 6:14

594

*For whom the LORD loveth he correcteth;
even as a father the son in whom he delighteth.*
PROVERBS 3:12

595

*The LORD is the portion of mine inheritance
and of my cup: thou maintainest my lot.*
PSALM 16:5

596

*His lord said unto him, Well done, thou good and faithful
servant: thou hast been faithful over a few things,
I will make thee ruler over many things:
enter thou into the joy of thy lord.*

MATTHEW 25:21

597

*For the Father himself loveth you, because ye have loved me,
and have believed that I came out from God.*

JOHN 16:27

598

*Wherefore seeing we also are compassed about with so great
a cloud of witnesses, let us lay aside every weight, and the sin
which doth so easily beset us, and let us run with patience the
race that is set before us, looking unto Jesus the author and
finisher of our faith; who for the joy that was set before him
endured the cross, despising the shame, and is set
down at the right hand of the throne of God.*

HEBREWS 12:1–2

599

*Yet if any man suffer as a Christian, let him not be ashamed;
but let him glorify God on this behalf.*

1 PETER 4:16

600

He hath dispersed, he hath given to the poor; his righteousness
endureth for ever; his horn shall be exalted with honour.
PSALM 112:9

601

When thou liest down, thou shalt not be afraid: yea,
thou shalt lie down, and thy sleep shall be sweet.
PROVERBS 3:24

602

I have seen an end of all perfection:
but thy commandment is exceeding broad.
PSALM 119:96

603

Till he fill thy mouth with laughing,
and thy lips with rejoicing.
JOB 8:21

604

For the LORD your God is he that goeth with you,
to fight for you against your enemies, to save you.
DEUTERONOMY 20:4

605

The earth and all the inhabitants thereof are dissolved:
I bear up the pillars of it.
PSALM 75:3

606

Then shall thy light break forth as the morning,
and thine health shall spring forth speedily:
and thy righteousness shall go before thee;
the glory of the LORD shall be thy reward.
ISAIAH 58:8

607

Keep therefore the words of this covenant,
and do them, that ye may prosper in all that ye do.
DEUTERONOMY 29:9

608

The spirit of a man will sustain his infirmity.
PROVERBS 18:14

609

Blessed are the meek: for they shall inherit the earth.
MATTHEW 5:5

610

The righteous shall flourish like the palm tree: he shall grow
like a cedar in Lebanon. Those that be planted in the house
of the LORD shall flourish in the courts of our God.
They shall still bring forth fruit in old age;
they shall be fat and flourishing.
PSALM 92:12–14

611

If ye know these things, happy are ye if ye do them.
JOHN 13:17

612

So then faith cometh by hearing,
and hearing by the word of God.
ROMANS 10:17

613

The LORD is on my side; I will not fear:
what can man do unto me?
PSALM 118:6

614

They that sow in tears shall reap in joy.
PSALM 126:5

615

But we all, with open face beholding as in a glass the
glory of the Lord, are changed into the same image from
glory to glory, even as by the Spirit of the Lord.
2 CORINTHIANS 3:18

616

I, even I, am he that comforteth you: who art thou,
that thou shouldest be afraid of a man that shall die,
and of the son of man which shall be made as grass.
ISAIAH 51:12

617

Of his own will begat he us with the word of truth,
that we should be a kind of firstfruits of his creatures.
JAMES 1:18

618

The LORD is my rock, and my fortress, and my deliverer;
my God, my strength, in whom I will trust; my buckler,
and the horn of my salvation, and my high tower.
PSALM 18:2

619

Commit thy way unto the LORD; trust also in him;
and he shall bring it to pass. And he shall bring forth thy
righteousness as the light, and thy judgment as the noonday.
PSALM 37:5–6

620

Wherefore we receiving a kingdom which cannot be moved,
let us have grace, whereby we may serve God
acceptably with reverence and godly fear.
HEBREWS 12:28

621

Ye are of God, little children, and have overcome them:
because greater is he that is in you, than he
that is in the world.
1 JOHN 4:4

622

For, brethren, ye have been called unto liberty;
only use not liberty for an occasion to the flesh,
but by love serve one another.
GALATIANS 5:13

623

And thou shalt do that which is right and good in the
sight of the LORD: that it may be well with thee,
and that thou mayest go in and possess the good
land which the LORD sware unto thy fathers.
DEUTERONOMY 6:18

624

And God shall wipe away all tears from their eyes;
and there shall be no more death, neither sorrow,
nor crying, neither shall there be any more pain:
for the former things are passed away.
REVELATION 21:4

625

Ah Lord GOD! behold, thou hast made the heaven
and the earth by thy great power and stretched
out arm, and there is nothing too hard for thee.
JEREMIAH 32:17

626

Be not wise in thine own eyes: fear the LORD,
and depart from evil. It shall be health to
thy navel, and marrow to thy bones.
PROVERBS 3:7–8

627

I will heal their backsliding, I will love them freely:
for mine anger is turned away from him.
HOSEA 14:4

628

Therefore my heart is glad, and my glory rejoiceth:
my flesh also shall rest in hope. For thou wilt not
leave my soul in hell; neither wilt thou suffer
thine Holy One to see corruption.
PSALM 16:9–10

629

Surely goodness and mercy shall follow me all the days of my
life: and I will dwell in the house of the LORD for ever.
PSALM 23:6

630

As for God, his way is perfect; the word of the LORD is tried:
he is a buckler to all them that trust in him.
2 SAMUEL 22:31

631

And the LORD shall help them, and deliver them:
he shall deliver them from the wicked, and save them,
because they trust in him.

PSALM 37:40

632

Blessed are the pure in heart: for they shall see God.
MATTHEW 5:8

633

For we have not an high priest which cannot be touched
with the feeling of our infirmities; but was in all points
tempted like as we are, yet without sin. Let us therefore
come boldly unto the throne of grace, that we may obtain
mercy, and find grace to help in time of need.

HEBREWS 4:15–16

634

Heaven and earth shall pass away:
but my words shall not pass away.
LUKE 21:33

635

Likewise, I say unto you, there is joy in the presence
of the angels of God over one sinner that repenteth.
LUKE 15:10

636

They that hate thee shall be clothed with shame;
and the dwelling place of the wicked shall come to nought.
JOB 8:22

637

Be not afraid of sudden fear, neither of the desolation of the
wicked, when it cometh. For the LORD shall be thy
confidence, and shall keep thy foot from being taken.
PROVERBS 3:25–26

638

Blessed are they that do his commandments, that they may
have right to the tree of life, and may enter
in through the gates into the city.
REVELATION 22:14

639

Who will render to every man according to his deeds:
to them who by patient continuance in well doing seek
for glory and honour and immortality, eternal life.
ROMANS 2:6–7

640

For I the LORD thy God will hold thy right hand,
saying unto thee, Fear not; I will help thee.
ISAIAH 41:13

641

They send forth their little ones like a flock,
and their children dance.
JOB 21:11

642

For the oppression of the poor, for the sighing of the needy,
now will I arise, saith the LORD; I will set him
in safety from him that puffeth at him.
PSALM 12:5

643

But thou, when thou prayest, enter into thy closet, and when
thou hast shut thy door, pray to thy Father which is in secret;
and thy Father which seeth in secret shall reward thee openly.
MATTHEW 6:6

644

For in the time of trouble he shall hide me in his pavilion:
in the secret of his tabernacle shall he hide me; he shall set
me up upon a rock. And now shall mine head be lifted
up above mine enemies round about me: therefore will
I offer in his tabernacle sacrifices of joy; I will sing,
yea, I will sing praises unto the LORD.
PSALM 27:5–6

645

See now that I, even I, am he, and there is no god with me:
I kill, and I make alive; I wound, and I heal: neither
is there any that can deliver out of my hand.

DEUTERONOMY 32:39

646

Are not five sparrows sold for two farthings, and not one of
them is forgotten before God? But even the very hairs of
your head are all numbered. Fear not therefore:
ye are of more value than many sparrows.

LUKE 12:6–7

647

But now being made free from sin, and become servants
to God, ye have your fruit unto holiness,
and the end everlasting life.

ROMANS 6:22

648

The hoary head is a crown of glory,
if it be found in the way of righteousness.

PROVERBS 16:31

649

The eyes of the LORD preserve knowledge,
and he overthroweth the words of the transgressor.

PROVERBS 22:12

650

Be not forgetful to entertain strangers:
for thereby some have entertained angels unawares.
HEBREWS 13:2

651

For there is hope of a tree, if it be cut down, that it will
sprout again, and that the tender branch
thereof will not cease.
JOB 14:7

652

Though he fall, he shall not be utterly cast down:
for the LORD upholdeth him with his hand.
PSALM 37:24

653

Unto thee, O my strength, will I sing:
for God is my defence, and the God of my mercy.
PSALM 59:17

654

I will bless the LORD, who hath given me counsel:
my reins also instruct me in the night seasons.
PSALM 16:7

655

*I exhort therefore, that, first of all, supplications, prayers,
intercessions, and giving of thanks, be made for all men;
for kings, and for all that are in authority; that we may
lead a quiet and peaceable life in all godliness and honesty.
For this is good and acceptable in the sight of God our
Saviour; who will have all men to be saved,
and to come unto the knowledge of the truth.*
1 Timothy 2:1–4

656

*For the eyes of the Lord run to and fro throughout the
whole earth, to shew himself strong in the behalf of them
whose heart is perfect toward him. Herein thou hast done
foolishly: therefore from henceforth thou shalt have wars.*
2 Chronicles 16:9

657

*Be ye mindful always of his covenant; the word which
he commanded to a thousand generations.*
1 Chronicles 16:15

658

*Yet the Lord will command his lovingkindness in the day
time, and in the night his song shall be with me,
and my prayer unto the God of my life.*
Psalm 42:8

659

He raiseth up the poor out of the dust,
and lifteth the needy out of the dunghill.
PSALM 113:7

660

And he arose, and rebuked the wind, and said unto
the sea, Peace, be still. And the wind ceased,
and there was a great calm.
MARK 4:39

661

For thou wilt light my candle: the LORD my
God will enlighten my darkness.
PSALM 18:28

662

But if the wicked will turn from all his sins that he hath
committed, and keep all my statutes, and do that which is
lawful and right, he shall surely live, he shall not die.
All his transgressions that he hath committed,
they shall not be mentioned unto him: in his
righteousness that he hath done he shall live.
EZEKIEL 18:21–22

663

Yea, though I walk through the valley of the shadow
of death, I will fear no evil: for thou art with me;
thy rod and thy staff they comfort me.

PSALM 23:4

664

Because of his strength will I wait upon thee: for God is
my defence. The God of my mercy shall prevent me:
God shall let me see my desire upon mine enemies.

PSALM 59:9–10

665

The righteous also shall hold on his way, and he that
hath clean hands shall be stronger and stronger.

JOB 17:9

666

Why art thou cast down, O my soul? and why art thou
disquieted within me? hope thou in God: for I shall yet
praise him, who is the health of my
countenance, and my God.

PSALM 42:11

667

He that walketh with wise men shall be wise:
but a companion of fools shall be destroyed.

PROVERBS 13:20

668

The LORD taketh my part with them that help me:
therefore shall I see my desire upon them that hate me.
PSALM 118:7

669

Thy word is true from the beginning: and every one
of thy righteous judgments endureth for ever.
PSALM 119:160

670

Blessed are the merciful: for they shall obtain mercy.
MATTHEW 5:7

671

And he said unto them, Why are ye troubled? and why do
thoughts arise in your hearts? Behold my hands and my feet,
that it is I myself: handle me, and see; for a spirit
hath not flesh and bones, as ye see me have.
LUKE 24:38–39

672

Therefore shall ye lay up these my words in your heart
and in your soul, and bind them for a sign upon your hand,
that they may be as frontlets between your eyes.
DEUTERONOMY 11:18

673

Jesus said unto him, If thou canst believe,
all things are possible to him that believeth.
MARK 9:23

674

Thy dead men shall live, together with my dead body shall
they arise. Awake and sing, ye that dwell in dust: for thy dew
is as the dew of herbs, and the earth shall cast out the dead.
ISAIAH 26:19

675

With the ancient is wisdom; and in length of days
understanding. With him is wisdom and strength,
he hath counsel and understanding.
JOB 12:12–13

676

He delivereth me from mine enemies: yea,
thou liftest me up above those that rise up against me:
thou hast delivered me from the violent man.
PSALM 18:48

677

Yea, let none that wait on thee be ashamed: let them be
ashamed which transgress without cause.
PSALM 25:3

678

For the wages of sin is death; but the gift of God
is eternal life through Jesus Christ our Lord.
ROMANS 6:23

679

For since by man came death, by man came
also the resurrection of the dead.
1 CORINTHIANS 15:21

680

And hath put all things under his feet,
and gave him to be the head over all things to the church.
EPHESIANS 1:22

681

Lord, who shall abide in thy tabernacle? who shall dwell
in thy holy hill? He that walketh uprightly, and worketh
righteousness, and speaketh the truth in his heart.
PSALM 15:1–2

682

For I will be merciful to their unrighteousness,
and their sins and their iniquities will I remember no more.
HEBREWS 8:12

683

In this was manifested the love of God toward us,
because that God sent his only begotten Son
into the world, that we might live through him.
1 JOHN 4:9

684

This I say then, Walk in the Spirit,
and ye shall not fulfil the lust of the flesh.
GALATIANS 5:16

685

I know both how to be abased, and I know how to abound:
every where and in all things I am instructed both to be full
and to be hungry, both to abound and to suffer need. I can do
all things through Christ which strengtheneth me.
PHILIPPIANS 4:12–13

686

The voice of rejoicing and salvation is in the tabernacles
of the righteous: the right hand of the LORD doeth valiantly.
PSALM 118:15

687

Surely he scorneth the scorners:
but he giveth grace unto the lowly.
PROVERBS 3:34

688

But the path of the just is as the shining light,
that shineth more and more unto the perfect day.
PROVERBS 4:18

689

Keep thy heart with all diligence;
for out of it are the issues of life.
PROVERBS 4:23

690

The entrance of thy words giveth light;
it giveth understanding unto the simple.
PSALM 119:130

691

In famine he shall redeem thee from death:
and in war from the power of the sword.
JOB 5:20

692

Glory and honour are in his presence;
strength and gladness are in his place.
1 CHRONICLES 16:27

693

*Our fathers trusted in thee: they trusted, and thou didst
deliver them. They cried unto thee, and were delivered:
they trusted in thee, and were not confounded.*

PSALM 22:4–5

694

*Which is come unto you, as it is in all the world; and bringeth
forth fruit, as it doth also in you, since the day ye heard of it,
and knew the grace of God in truth.*

COLOSSIANS 1:6

695

*Lead me in thy truth, and teach me: for thou art
the God of my salvation; on thee do I wait all the day.*

PSALM 25:5

696

*Who is a God like unto thee, that pardoneth iniquity,
and passeth by the transgression of the remnant of his
heritage? he retaineth not his anger for ever, because he
delighteth in mercy. He will turn again, he will have
compassion upon us; he will subdue our iniquities;
and thou wilt cast all their sins into the depths of the sea.*

MICAH 7:18–19

697

Let, I pray thee, thy merciful kindness be for my comfort,
according to thy word unto thy servant.
PSALM 119:76

698

Where no counsel is, the people fall:
but in the multitude of counsellors there is safety.
PROVERBS 11:14

699

The LORD our God be with us, as he was with our fathers:
let him not leave us, nor forsake us.
1 KINGS 8:57

700

And in every work that he began in the service of the house
of God, and in the law, and in the commandments, to seek his
God, he did it with all his heart, and prospered.
2 CHRONICLES 31:21

701

I am the LORD: that is my name: and my glory will I not give
to another, neither my praise to graven images. Behold,
the former things are come to pass, and new things do
I declare: before they spring forth I tell you of them.
ISAIAH 42:8–9

702

That they might set their hope in God,
and not forget the works of God.
PSALM 78:7

703

Submit yourselves therefore to God.
Resist the devil, and he will flee from you.
JAMES 4:7

704

For then shalt thou have thy delight in the Almighty,
and shalt lift up thy face unto God.
JOB 22:26

705

For every one that asketh receiveth; and he that seeketh
findeth; and to him that knocketh it shall be opened.
MATTHEW 7:8

706

The light of the eyes rejoiceth the heart:
and a good report maketh the bones fat.
PROVERBS 15:30

707

Behold, the heaven and the heaven of heavens is the LORD's
thy God, the earth also, with all that therein is.

DEUTERONOMY 10:14

708

For thus saith the Lord GOD, the Holy One of Israel;
In returning and rest shall ye be saved; in quietness
and in confidence shall be your strength: and ye would not.

ISAIAH 30:15

709

The LORD hath chastened me sore:
but he hath not given me over unto death.

PSALM 118:18

710

The LORD shall reign for ever, even thy God,
O Zion, unto all generations. Praise ye the LORD.

PSALM 146:10

711

Blessed is he that readeth, and they that hear the words
of this prophecy, and keep those things which
are written therein: for the time is at hand.

REVELATION 1:3

712

And we know that the Son of God is come, and hath given us an understanding, that we may know him that is true, and we are in him that is true, even in his Son Jesus Christ. This is the true God, and eternal life.

1 John 5:20

713

The meek shall eat and be satisfied: they shall praise the Lord that seek him: your heart shall live for ever.

Psalm 22:26

714

And thou, Solomon my son, know thou the God of thy father, and serve him with a perfect heart and with a willing mind: for the Lord searcheth all hearts, and understandeth all the imaginations of the thoughts: if thou seek him, he will be found of thee; but if thou forsake him, he will cast thee off for ever.

1 Chronicles 28:9

715

*And it came to pass in process of time, that the king of
Egypt died: and the children of Israel sighed by reason of the
bondage, and they cried, and their cry came up unto God by
reason of the bondage. And God heard their groaning,
and God remembered his covenant with Abraham,
with Isaac, and with Jacob. And God looked upon
the children of Israel, and God had respect unto them.*
EXODUS 2:23–25

716

*I have been young, and now am old; yet have I not seen
the righteous forsaken, nor his seed begging bread.*
PSALM 37:25

717

*Blessed are the peacemakers:
for they shall be called the children of God.*
MATTHEW 5:9

718

*Let no man deceive himself. If any man among you seemeth
to be wise in this world, let him become a fool, that he may
be wise. For the wisdom of this world is foolishness with God.
For it is written, He taketh the wise in their own craftiness.*
1 CORINTHIANS 3:18–19

719

Wherefore take unto you the whole armour of God,
that ye may be able to withstand in the evil day,
and having done all, to stand.

EPHESIANS 6:13

720

For he hath not despised nor abhorred the affliction of
the afflicted; neither hath he hid his face from him;
but when he cried unto him, he heard.

PSALM 22:24

721

But I will deliver thee in that day, saith the LORD:
and thou shalt not be given into the hand of the men of
whom thou art afraid. For I will surely deliver thee,
and thou shalt not fall by the sword, but thy life
shall be for a prey unto thee: because thou hast
put thy trust in me, saith the LORD.

JEREMIAH 39:17–18

722

For I the LORD thy God will hold thy right hand,
saying unto thee, Fear not; I will help thee.

ISAIAH 41:13

723

And of his fulness have all we received, and grace for grace.
For the law was given by Moses, but grace and
truth came by Jesus Christ.
JOHN 1:16–17

724

He shall call upon me, and I will answer him: I will be
with him in trouble; I will deliver him, and honour him.
PSALM 91:15

725

He is ever merciful, and lendeth; and his seed is blessed.
PSALM 37:26

726

If we say that we have no sin, we deceive ourselves,
and the truth is not in us. If we confess our sins,
he is faithful and just to forgive us our sins,
and to cleanse us from all unrighteousness.
1 JOHN 1:8–9

727

And that from a child thou hast known the holy scriptures,
which are able to make thee wise unto salvation
through faith which is in Christ Jesus.
2 TIMOTHY 3:15

728

*O that there were such an heart in them, that they would fear
me, and keep all my commandments always, that it might
be well with them, and with their children for ever!*

DEUTERONOMY 5:29

729

*Behold, happy is the man whom God correcteth: therefore despise
not thou the chastening of the Almighty: for he maketh sore,
and bindeth up: he woundeth, and his hands make whole.*

JOB 5:17–18

730

*Mark the perfect man, and behold the upright:
for the end of that man is peace.*

PSALM 37:37

731

*My covenant will I not break,
nor alter the thing that is gone out of my lips.*

PSALM 89:34

732

*The LORD is my shepherd; I shall not want. He maketh me
to lie down in green pastures: he leadeth me beside the still
waters. He restoreth my soul: he leadeth me in the
paths of righteousness for his name's sake.*

PSALM 23:1–3

733

But now thus saith the Lord that created thee, O Jacob,
and he that formed thee, O Israel, Fear not: for I have
redeemed thee, I have called thee by thy name; thou art mine.

ISAIAH 43:1

734

Whoso eateth my flesh, and drinketh my blood,
hath eternal life; and I will raise him up at the last day.

JOHN 6:54

735

Peace I leave with you, my peace I give unto you:
not as the world giveth, give I unto you. Let not your
heart be troubled, neither let it be afraid.

JOHN 14:27

736

There is therefore now no condemnation to them which are in
Christ Jesus, who walk not after the flesh, but after the Spirit.

ROMANS 8:1

737

These things I have spoken unto you, that in me ye might
have peace. In the world ye shall have tribulation:
but be of good cheer; I have overcome the world.

JOHN 16:33

738

Am I a God at hand, saith the LORD, *and not a God*
afar off? Can any hide himself in secret places that
I shall not see him? saith the LORD. *Do not I*
fill heaven and earth? saith the LORD.

JEREMIAH 23:23–24

739

For this is my blood of the new testament,
which is shed for many for the remission of sins.

MATTHEW 26:28

740

But the anointing which ye have received of him abideth
in you, and ye need not that any man teach you: but as the
same anointing teacheth you of all things, and is truth, and is
no lie, and even as it hath taught you, ye shall abide in him.

1 JOHN 2:27

741

I am come a light into the world,
that whosoever believeth on me should not abide in darkness.

JOHN 12:46

742

*And he said, It is a light thing that thou shouldest be my
servant to raise up the tribes of Jacob, and to restore
the preserved of Israel: I will also give thee for a
light to the Gentiles, that thou mayest be
my salvation unto the end of the earth.*

ISAIAH 49:6

743

*If any of thine be driven out unto the outmost parts of
heaven, from thence will the LORD thy God
gather thee, and from thence will he fetch thee.*

DEUTERONOMY 30:4

744

*The LORD is my light and my salvation; whom shall I fear?
the LORD is the strength of my life; of whom shall I be afraid?
When the wicked, even mine enemies and my foes, came upon
me to eat up my flesh, they stumbled and fell. Though an host
should encamp against me, my heart shall not fear: though
war should rise against me, in this will I be confident.*

PSALM 27:1–3

745

*If ye abide in me, and my words abide in you,
ye shall ask what ye will, and it shall be done unto you.*

JOHN 15:7

746

And the Lord said, If ye had faith as a grain of mustard seed,
ye might say unto this sycamine tree, Be thou plucked
up by the root, and be thou planted in
the sea; and it should obey you.

LUKE 17:6

747

And the peace of God, which passeth all understanding,
shall keep your hearts and minds through Christ Jesus.

PHILIPPIANS 4:7

748

And thine ears shall hear a word behind thee, saying,
This is the way, walk ye in it, when ye turn
to the right hand, and when ye turn to the left.

ISAIAH 30:21

749

For the ways of man are before the eyes of the LORD,
and he pondereth all his goings.

PROVERBS 5:21

750

For the commandment is a lamp; and the law is light;
and reproofs of instruction are the way of life.

PROVERBS 6:23

751

*But whoso looketh into the perfect law of liberty, and
continueth therein, he being not a forgetful hearer,
but a doer of the work, this man shall be blessed in his deed.*
JAMES 1:25

752

*For the grace of God that bringeth salvation hath appeared
to all men, teaching us that, denying ungodliness and
worldly lusts, we should live soberly, righteously,
and godly, in this present world.*
TITUS 2:11–12

753

*He that hath my commandments, and keepeth them, he it is
that loveth me: and he that loveth me shall be loved of my
Father, and I will love him, and will manifest myself to him.*
JOHN 14:21

754

*Children's children are the crown of old men;
and the glory of children are their fathers.*
PROVERBS 17:6

755

*He hath made every thing beautiful in his time: also he hath
set the world in their heart, so that no man can find out the
work that God maketh from the beginning to the end.*

ECCLESIASTES 3:11

756

A sound heart is the life of the flesh.

PROVERBS 14:30

757

*Labour not for the meat which perisheth, but for that meat
which endureth unto everlasting life, which the Son of man
shall give unto you: for him hath God the Father sealed.*

JOHN 6:27

758

*And let us not be weary in well doing: for in due
season we shall reap, if we faint not.*

GALATIANS 6:9

759

*And as it is appointed unto men once to die, but after this the
judgment: so Christ was once offered to bear the sins of many;
and unto them that look for him shall he appear the
second time without sin unto salvation.*

HEBREWS 9:27–28

760

He that cometh from above is above all: he that is of the earth
is earthly, and speaketh of the earth: he that cometh
from heaven is above all.
JOHN 3:31

761

Depart from evil, and do good; and dwell for evermore.
For the LORD loveth judgment, and forsaketh not
his saints; they are preserved for ever:
but the seed of the wicked shall be cut off.
PSALM 37:27–28

762

And righteousness shall be the girdle of his loins,
and faithfulness the girdle of his reins.
ISAIAH 11:5

763

A merry heart doeth good like a medicine.
PROVERBS 17:22

764

He that tilleth his land shall have plenty of bread:
but he that followeth after vain persons
shall have poverty enough.
PROVERBS 28:19

765

Arise therefore, and get thee down, and go with them,
doubting nothing: for I have sent them.
ACTS 10:20

766

But as it is written, Eye hath not seen, nor ear heard,
neither have entered into the heart of man, the things
which God hath prepared for them that love him.
1 CORINTHIANS 2:9

767

Forasmuch then as the children are partakers of flesh and
blood, he also himself likewise took part of the same;
that through death he might destroy him that had the power
of death, that is, the devil; and deliver them who through
fear of death were all their lifetime subject to bondage.
HEBREWS 2:14–15

768

For wisdom is better than rubies; and all the things
that may be desired are not to be compared to it.
PROVERBS 8:11

769

Trouble and anguish have taken hold on me: yet thy
commandments are my delights.
PSALM 119:143

770

He that believeth on me, as the scripture hath said,
out of his belly shall flow rivers of living water.
JOHN 7:38

771

Thou shalt not be afraid of them: but shalt well remember what
the LORD thy God did unto Pharaoh, and unto all Egypt.
DEUTERONOMY 7:18

772

Keep my commandments, and live;
and my law as the apple of thine eye.
PROVERBS 7:2

773

Whosoever therefore shall break one of these least
commandments, and shall teach men so, he shall be called
the least in the kingdom of heaven: but whosoever shall
do and teach them, the same shall be called
great in the kingdom of heaven.
MATTHEW 5:19

774

Blessed is the man whose strength is in thee; in whose heart
are the ways of them. Who passing through the valley
of Baca make it a well; the rain also filleth the pools.
PSALM 84:5–6

775

I will be as the dew unto Israel: he shall grow
as the lily, and cast forth his roots as Lebanon.
HOSEA 14:5

776

Give instruction to a wise man, and he will be yet wiser:
teach a just man, and he will increase in learning.
PROVERBS 9:9

777

He becometh poor that dealeth with a slack hand:
but the hand of the diligent maketh rich.
PROVERBS 10:4

778

And the light shineth in darkness;
and the darkness comprehended it not.
JOHN 1:5

779

But thou shalt remember the LORD thy God: for it is he
that giveth thee power to get wealth, that he may establish
his covenant which he sware unto thy fathers, as it is this day.
DEUTERONOMY 8:18

780

If we believe not, yet he abideth faithful:
he cannot deny himself.
2 TIMOTHY 2:13

781

And my people shall dwell in a peaceable habitation,
and in sure dwellings, and in quiet resting places.
ISAIAH 32:18

782

Whom having not seen, ye love; in whom, though now ye
see him not, yet believing, ye rejoice with joy unspeakable
and full of glory: receiving the end of your faith,
even the salvation of your souls.
1 PETER 1:8–9

783

And he sat down, and called the twelve, and saith unto
them, If any man desire to be first, the same shall
be last of all, and servant of all.
MARK 9:35

784

It is the spirit that quickeneth; the flesh profiteth nothing:
the words that I speak unto you, they are spirit,
and they are life.
JOHN 6:63

785

He that is slow to anger is better than the mighty;
and he that ruleth his spirit than he that taketh a city.
PROVERBS 16:32

786

A man's pride shall bring him low:
but honour shall uphold the humble in spirit.
PROVERBS 29:23

787

We are troubled on every side, yet not distressed;
we are perplexed, but not in despair; persecuted,
but not forsaken; cast down, but not destroyed.
2 CORINTHIANS 4:8–9

788

For ye had compassion of me in my bonds, and took joyfully
the spoiling of your goods, knowing in yourselves that ye
have in heaven a better and an enduring substance.
HEBREWS 10:34

789

I will hear what God the LORD will speak: for he will
speak peace unto his people, and to his saints:
but let them not turn again to folly.
PSALM 85:8

790

And it shall come to pass, if ye shall hearken diligently unto my commandments which I command you this day, to love the LORD your God, and to serve him with all your heart and with all your soul, that I will give you the rain of your land in his due season, the first rain and the latter rain, that thou mayest gather in thy corn, and thy wine, and thine oil. And I will send grass in thy fields for thy cattle, that thou mayest eat and be full.

DEUTERONOMY 11:13–15

791

Although the fig tree shall not blossom, neither shall fruit be in the vines; the labour of the olive shall fail, and the fields shall yield no meat; the flock shall be cut off from the fold, and there shall be no herd in the stalls: yet I will rejoice in the LORD, I will joy in the God of my salvation.

HABAKKUK 3:17–18

792

He that hath pity upon the poor lendeth unto the LORD; and that which he hath given will he pay him again.

PROVERBS 19:17

793

*Lift up your eyes on high, and behold who hath created
these things, that bringeth out their host by number:
he calleth them all by names by the greatness of his might,
for that he is strong in power; not one faileth.*

ISAIAH 40:26

794

*Henceforth there is laid up for me a crown of righteousness,
which the Lord, the righteous judge, shall give me at that day:
and not to me only, but unto all them also that love his appearing.*

2 TIMOTHY 4:8

795

*And the fruit of righteousness is sown
in peace of them that make peace.*

JAMES 3:18

796

*Better is an handful with quietness, than both the
hands full with travail and vexation of spirit.*

ECCLESIASTES 4:6

797

*The fear of the LORD tendeth to life: and he that hath
it shall abide satisfied; he shall not be visited with evil.*

PROVERBS 19:23

798

He that giveth unto the poor shall not lack:
but he that hideth his eyes shall have many a curse.
PROVERBS 28:27

799

He that walketh righteously, and speaketh uprightly; he that
despiseth the gain of oppressions, that shaketh his hands from
holding of bribes, that stoppeth his ears from hearing of blood,
and shutteth his eyes from seeing evil; he shall dwell on high:
his place of defence shall be the munitions of rocks: bread shall
be given him; his waters shall be sure.
ISAIAH 33:15–16

800

Thou shalt make thy prayer unto him,
and he shall hear thee, and thou shalt pay thy vows.
JOB 22:27

801

Then will I sprinkle clean water upon you, and ye shall be clean:
from all your filthiness, and from all your idols, will I cleanse you.
EZEKIEL 36:25

802

Blessed are they which are persecuted for righteousness'
sake: for theirs is the kingdom of heaven.
MATTHEW 5:10

803

*And the Levite, (because he hath no part nor inheritance
with thee,) and the stranger, and the fatherless,
and the widow, which are within thy gates, shall come,
and shall eat and be satisfied; that the LORD thy God may
bless thee in all the work of thine hand which thou doest.*

DEUTERONOMY 14:29

804

*He that believeth on the Son hath everlasting life:
and he that believeth not the Son shall not see life;
but the wrath of God abideth on him.*

JOHN 3:36

805

*Abide in me, and I in you. As the branch cannot bear
fruit of itself, except it abide in the vine; no more can ye,
except ye abide in me. I am the vine, ye are the branches:
he that abideth in me, and I in him, the same bringeth
forth much fruit: for without me ye can do nothing.*

JOHN 15:4–5

806

*He that spared not his own Son, but delivered him up
for us all, how shall he not with him also
freely give us all things?*

ROMANS 8:32

807

For as the rain cometh down, and the snow from heaven,
and returneth not thither, but watereth the earth,
and maketh it bring forth and bud, that it may give
seed to the sower, and bread to the eater: so shall my word
be that goeth forth out of my mouth: it shall not return
unto me void, but it shall accomplish that which I please,
and it shall prosper in the thing whereto I sent it.

ISAIAH 55:10–11

808

The thoughts of the diligent tend only to plenteousness;
but of every one that is hasty only to want.

PROVERBS 21:5

809

When thou passest through the waters, I will be with thee;
and through the rivers, they shall not overflow thee: when
thou walkest through the fire, thou shalt not be burned;
neither shall the flame kindle upon thee.

ISAIAH 43:2

810

The God of my rock; in him will I trust: he is my shield,
and the horn of my salvation, my high tower,
and my refuge, my saviour; thou savest me from violence.

2 SAMUEL 22:3

811

*That I may cause those that love me to
inherit substance; and I will fill their treasures.*
PROVERBS 8:21

812

*O satisfy us early with thy mercy;
that we may rejoice and be glad all our days.*
PSALM 90:14

813

*Let your conversation be without covetousness;
and be content with such things as ye have: for he hath said,
I will never leave thee, nor forsake thee.*
HEBREWS 13:5

814

*Now our Lord Jesus Christ himself, and God, even our
Father, which hath loved us, and hath given us everlasting
consolation and good hope through grace, comfort your
hearts, and stablish you in every good word and work.*
2 THESSALONIANS 2:16–17

815

*I love them that love me; and those that seek me early shall
find me. Riches and honour are with me; yea, durable riches
and righteousness. My fruit is better than gold, yea,
than fine gold; and my revenue than choice silver.*
PROVERBS 8:17–19

816

And I will put my spirit within you, and cause you to walk
in my statutes, and ye shall keep my judgments, and do them.
EZEKIEL 36:27

817

Say not thou, I will recompense evil;
but wait on the LORD, and he shall save thee.
PROVERBS 20:22

818

He shall cover thee with his feathers, and under his wings
shalt thou trust: his truth shall be thy shield and buckler.
PSALM 91:4

819

And this is the Father's will which hath sent me, that of all
which he hath given me I should lose nothing, but should raise it
up again at the last day. And this is the will of him that sent me,
that every one which seeth the Son, and believeth on him,
may have everlasting life: and I will raise him up at the last day.
JOHN 6:39–40

820

And, behold, I come quickly; and my reward is with me,
to give every man according as his work shall be. I am Alpha
and Omega, the beginning and the end, the first and the last.
REVELATION 22:12–13

821

Correct thy son, and he shall give thee rest; yea,
he shall give delight unto thy soul.

PROVERBS 29:17

822

Since thou wast precious in my sight, thou hast been
honourable, and I have loved thee: therefore will I
give men for thee, and people for thy life.

ISAIAH 43:4

823

And now, brethren, I commend you to God, and to the word
of his grace, which is able to build you up, and to give you
an inheritance among all them which are sanctified.

ACTS 20:32

824

And his mercy is on them that fear
him from generation to generation.

LUKE 1:50

825

And all these blessings shall come on thee, and overtake thee,
if thou shalt hearken unto the voice of the LORD thy God.
Blessed shalt thou be in the city, and blessed shalt thou be in
the field. Blessed shall be the fruit of thy body, and the fruit
of thy ground, and the fruit of thy cattle, the increase of thy
kine, and the flocks of thy sheep. Blessed shall be thy basket
and thy store. Blessed shalt thou be when thou comest in,
and blessed shalt thou be when thou goest out.
DEUTERONOMY 28:2–6

826

Let your light so shine before men, that they may see your
good works, and glorify your Father which is in heaven.
MATTHEW 5:16

827

Fear none of those things which thou shalt suffer: behold,
the devil shall cast some of you into prison, that ye may be
tried; and ye shall have tribulation ten days: be thou faithful
unto death, and I will give thee a crown of life.
REVELATION 2:10

828

For whom the Lord loveth he chasteneth, and scourgeth
every son whom he receiveth. If ye endure chastening,
God dealeth with you as with sons; for what
son is he whom the father chasteneth not?
HEBREWS 12:6–7

829

By humility and the fear of the LORD are riches,
and honour, and life.

PROVERBS 22:4

830

That he would grant unto us, that we being delivered out
of the hand of our enemies might serve him without fear.

LUKE 1:74

831

For the kingdom of God is not meat and drink; but
righteousness, and peace, and joy in the Holy Ghost.

ROMANS 14:17

832

But the salvation of the righteous is of the LORD:
he is their strength in the time of trouble.

PSALM 37:39

833

And when he was come into the house, the blind men came
to him: and Jesus saith unto them, Believe ye that I am able to
do this? They said unto him, Yea, Lord. Then touched
he their eyes, saying, According to your faith be it unto you.
And their eyes were opened; and Jesus straitly charged
them, saying, See that no man know it.

MATTHEW 9:28–30

834

For whatsoever is born of God overcometh the world:
and this is the victory that overcometh
the world, even our faith.

1 JOHN 5:4

835

The meek also shall increase their joy in the LORD,
and the poor among men shall rejoice
in the Holy One of Israel.

ISAIAH 29:19

836

And the LORD shall make thee the head, and not the tail;
and thou shalt be above only, and thou shalt not be beneath;
if that thou hearken unto the commandments of the LORD
thy God, which I command thee this day,
to observe and to do them.

DEUTERONOMY 28:13

837

Have not I commanded thee? Be strong and of a
good courage; be not afraid, neither be thou dismayed:
for the LORD thy God is with thee whithersoever thou goest.

JOSHUA 1:9

838

Pleasant words are as an honeycomb,
sweet to the soul, and health to the bones.
PROVERBS 16:24

839

The wicked plotteth against the just, and gnasheth upon
him with his teeth. The LORD shall laugh at him:
for he seeth that his day is coming.
PSALM 37:12–13

840

And whatsoever ye shall ask in my name, that will I do,
that the Father may be glorified in the Son.
If ye shall ask any thing in my name, I will do it.
JOHN 14:13–14

841

And shall not God avenge his own elect, which cry day
and night unto him, though he bear long with them?
LUKE 18:7

842

For in thee, O LORD, do I hope: thou wilt hear, O Lord my God.
PSALM 38:15

843

While we look not at the things which are seen, but at the things which are not seen: for the things which are seen are temporal; but the things which are not seen are eternal.

2 CORINTHIANS 4:18

844

Even the youths shall faint and be weary, and the young men shall utterly fall: but they that wait upon the LORD shall renew their strength; they shall mount up with wings as eagles; they shall run, and not be weary; and they shall walk, and not faint.

ISAIAH 40:30–31

845

Call unto me, and I will answer thee, and show thee great and mighty things, which thou knowest not.

JEREMIAH 33:3

846

All scripture is given by inspiration of God, and is profitable for doctrine, for reproof, for correction, for instruction in righteousness: that the man of God may be perfect, thoroughly furnished unto all good works.

2 TIMOTHY 3:16–17

847

Behold, we count them happy which endure. Ye have heard of
the patience of Job, and have seen the end of the Lord;
that the Lord is very pitiful, and of tender mercy.
JAMES 5:11

848

When a man's ways please the LORD, he maketh even
his enemies to be at peace with him.
PROVERBS 16:7

849

We have also a more sure word of prophecy; whereunto ye do
well that ye take heed, as unto a light that shineth in a dark
place, until the day dawn, and the day star arise in your hearts.
2 PETER 1:19

850

And as Moses lifted up the serpent in the wilderness,
even so must the Son of man be lifted up: that whosoever
believeth in him should not perish, but have eternal life.
JOHN 3:14–15

851

For he hath made him to be sin for us, who knew no sin;
that we might be made the righteousness of God in him.
2 CORINTHIANS 5:21

852

*He that dwelleth in the secret place of the most
High shall abide under the shadow of the Almighty.
I will say of the LORD, He is my refuge and
my fortress: my God; in him will I trust.*

PSALM 91:1–2

853

*For a just man falleth seven times, and riseth up again:
but the wicked shall fall into mischief.*

PROVERBS 24:16

854

*Wherefore gird up the loins of your mind, be sober,
and hope to the end for the grace that is to be brought
unto you at the revelation of Jesus Christ.*

1 PETER 1:13

855

*For every creature of God is good, and nothing to be refused,
if it be received with thanksgiving.*

1 TIMOTHY 4:4

856

Behold, all they that were incensed against thee shall be
ashamed and confounded: they shall be as nothing;
and they that strive with thee shall perish. Thou shalt seek
them, and shalt not find them, even them that contended
with thee: they that war against thee shall be
as nothing, and as a thing of nought.
ISAIAH 41:11–12

857

Train up a child in the way he should go:
and when he is old, he will not depart from it.
PROVERBS 22:6

858

For thus saith the LORD, That after seventy years be
accomplished at Babylon I will visit you, and perform my
good word toward you, in causing you to return to this place.
For I know the thoughts that I think toward you,
saith the LORD, thoughts of peace, and not of evil,
to give you an expected end.
JEREMIAH 29:10–11

859

Cast thy bread upon the waters:
for thou shalt find it after many days.
ECCLESIASTES 11:1

860

*And thou shalt return and obey the voice of the LORD,
and do all his commandments which I command thee this
day. And the LORD thy God will make thee plenteous in
every work of thine hand, in the fruit of thy body,
and in the fruit of thy cattle, and in the fruit of thy
land, for good: for the LORD will again rejoice
over thee for good, as he rejoiced over thy fathers.*

DEUTERONOMY 30:8–9

861

*And this is the record, that God hath given to us
eternal life, and this life is in his Son.*

1 JOHN 5:11

862

*And he went out to meet Asa, and said unto him, Hear ye
me, Asa, and all Judah and Benjamin; The LORD is with
you, while ye be with him; and if ye seek him, he will be
found of you; but if ye forsake him, he will forsake you.*

2 CHRONICLES 15:2

863

*Behold my servant, whom I uphold; mine elect, in whom my
soul delighteth; I have put my spirit upon him: he shall bring
forth judgment to the Gentiles. He shall not cry, nor lift up,
nor cause his voice to be heard in the street. A bruised reed
shall he not break, and the smoking flax shall he not quench:
he shall bring forth judgment unto truth. He shall not fail
nor be discouraged, till he have set judgment in the
earth: and the isles shall wait for his law.*

Isaiah 42:1–4

864

*The fear of man bringeth a snare:
but whoso putteth his trust in the Lord shall be safe.*

Proverbs 29:25

865

*Thou shalt also decree a thing, and it shall be established
unto thee: and the light shall shine upon thy ways.*

Job 22:28

866

*These things have I written unto you that believe on the name
of the Son of God; that ye may know that ye have eternal life,
and that ye may believe on the name of the Son of God.*

1 John 5:13

867

For God sent not his Son into the world to condemn the world; but that the world through him might be saved.
JOHN 3:17

868

For he shall deliver the needy when he crieth; the poor also, and him that hath no helper. He shall spare the poor and needy, and shall save the souls of the needy.
PSALM 72:12–13

869

The LORD knoweth the days of the upright: and their inheritance shall be for ever.
PSALM 37:18

870

Then shalt thou call, and the LORD shall answer; thou shalt cry, and he shall say, Here I am. If thou take away from the midst of thee the yoke, the putting forth of the finger, and speaking vanity.
ISAIAH 58:9

871

And Moses said unto the people, Fear ye not, stand still, and see the salvation of the LORD, which he will shew to you to day: for the Egyptians whom ye have seen to day, ye shall see them again no more for ever. The LORD shall fight for you, and ye shall hold your peace.

EXODUS 14:13–14

872

*Thou art my hiding place and my shield:
I hope in thy word.*

PSALM 119:114

873

Then spake Jesus again unto them, saying, I am the light of the world: he that followeth me shall not walk in darkness, but shall have the light of life.

JOHN 8:12

874

For whosoever shall give you a cup of water to drink in my name, because ye belong to Christ, verily I say unto you, he shall not lose his reward.

MARK 9:41

875

And David said to Solomon his son, Be strong and of good courage, and do it: fear not, nor be dismayed: for the LORD God, even my God, will be with thee; he will not fail thee, nor forsake thee, until thou hast finished all the work for the service of the house of the LORD.

1 CHRONICLES 28:20

876

For they verily for a few days chastened us after their own pleasure; but he for our profit, that we might be partakers of his holiness. Now no chastening for the present seemeth to be joyous, but grievous: nevertheless afterward it yieldeth the peaceable fruit of righteousness unto them which are exercised thereby.

HEBREWS 12:10–11

877

My doctrine shall drop as the rain, my speech shall distil as the dew, as the small rain upon the tender herb, and as the showers upon the grass.

DEUTERONOMY 32:2

878

Blessed is the people that know the joyful sound: they shall walk, O LORD, in the light of thy countenance. In thy name shall they rejoice all the day: and in thy righteousness shall they be exalted.

PSALM 89:15–16

879

Hast thou faith? have it to thyself before God. Happy is he
that condemneth not himself in that thing which he alloweth.
ROMANS 14:22

880

If thine enemy be hungry, give him bread to eat; and if he
be thirsty, give him water to drink: for thou shalt heap coals
of fire upon his head, and the LORD shall reward thee.
PROVERBS 25:21–22

881

And if thou draw out thy soul to the hungry, and satisfy the
afflicted soul; then shall thy light rise in obscurity,
and thy darkness be as the noon day.
ISAIAH 58:10

882

(For we walk by faith, not by sight:) we are confident,
I say, and willing rather to be absent from the
body, and to be present with the Lord.
2 CORINTHIANS 5:7–8

883

I have many things to say and to judge of you: but he that
sent me is true; and I speak to the world those
things which I have heard of him.
JOHN 8:26

884

He delivereth the poor in his affliction,
and openeth their ears in oppression.
JOB 36:15

885

And he said unto them, Verily I say unto you, There is no
man that hath left house, or parents, or brethren, or wife,
or children, for the kingdom of God's sake, who shall
not receive manifold more in this present time,
and in the world to come life everlasting.
LUKE 18:29–30

886

For he that soweth to his flesh shall of the flesh reap
corruption; but he that soweth to the Spirit
shall of the Spirit reap life everlasting.
GALATIANS 6:8

887

And refused to obey, neither were mindful of thy wonders
that thou didst among them; but hardened their necks, and in
their rebellion appointed a captain to return to their bondage:
but thou art a God ready to pardon, gracious and merciful,
slow to anger, and of great kindness, and forsookest them not.
NEHEMIAH 9:17

888

I waited patiently for the LORD; and he inclined unto me,
and heard my cry. He brought me up also out of an horrible
pit, out of the miry clay, and set my feet upon a rock,
and established my goings. And he hath put a new song
in my mouth, even praise unto our God: many shall
see it, and fear, and shall trust in the LORD.
PSALM 40:1–3

889

Thy word is a lamp unto my feet,
and a light unto my path.
PSALM 119:105

890

Blessed are ye, when men shall revile you, and persecute
you, and shall say all manner of evil against you falsely,
for my sake. Rejoice, and be exceeding glad: for great
is your reward in heaven: for so persecuted they
the prophets which were before you.
MATTHEW 5:11–12

891

But the LORD your God ye shall fear;
and he shall deliver you out of the hand of all your enemies.
2 KINGS 17:39

892

Now therefore hearken unto me, O ye children:
for blessed are they that keep my ways.
Hear instruction, and be wise, and refuse it not.
PROVERBS 8:32–33

893

To appoint unto them that mourn in Zion, to give unto them
beauty for ashes, the oil of joy for mourning, the garment of
praise for the spirit of heaviness; that they might be called
trees of righteousness, the planting of the LORD,
that he might be glorified.
ISAIAH 61:3

894

Be afflicted, and mourn, and weep: let your laughter
be turned to mourning, and your joy to heaviness.
Humble yourselves in the sight of the
Lord, and he shall lift you up.
JAMES 4:9–10

895

And this is the confidence that we have in him, that,
if we ask any thing according to his will, he heareth us:
and if we know that he hear us, whatsoever we ask,
we know that we have the petitions that we desired of him.
1 JOHN 5:14–15

896

Where there is no vision, the people perish:
but he that keepeth the law, happy is he.
PROVERBS 29:18

897

Jesus said unto her, I am the resurrection, and the life:
he that believeth in me, though he were dead, yet shall
he live: and whosoever liveth and believeth
in me shall never die. Believest thou this?
JOHN 11:25–26

898

Nevertheless God, that comforteth those that are
cast down, comforted us by the coming of Titus.
2 CORINTHIANS 7:6

899

Even the mystery which hath been hid from ages
and from generations, but now is made manifest to his
saints: to whom God would make known what is
the riches of the glory of this mystery among the
Gentiles; which is Christ in you, the hope of glory.
COLOSSIANS 1:26–27

900

When men are cast down, then thou shalt say,
There is lifting up; and he shall save the humble person.
JOB 22:29

901

If his children forsake my law, and walk not in my judgments;
if they break my statutes, and keep not my commandments;
then will I visit their transgression with the rod, and their
iniquity with stripes. Nevertheless my lovingkindness will I
not utterly take from him, nor suffer my faithfulness to fail.
PSALM 89:30–33

902

Before I formed thee in the belly I knew thee; and before thou
camest forth out of the womb I sanctified thee.
JEREMIAH 1:5

903

There is that scattereth, and yet increaseth; and there is
that withholdeth more than is meet, but it tendeth to
poverty. The liberal soul shall be made fat: and he
that watereth shall be watered also himself.
PROVERBS 11:24–25

904

And the prayer of faith shall save the sick, and the Lord
shall raise him up; and if he have committed sins,
they shall be forgiven him.
JAMES 5:15

905

*For we brought nothing into this world, and it is
certain we can carry nothing out. And having food
and raiment let us be therewith content.*

1 TIMOTHY 6:7–8

906

*As for me, this is my covenant with them, saith the LORD;
My spirit that is upon thee, and my words which I have put
in thy mouth, shall not depart out of thy mouth, nor out of
the mouth of thy seed, nor out of the mouth of thy seed's
seed, saith the LORD, from henceforth and for ever.*

ISAIAH 59:21

907

*The LORD is nigh unto all them that call upon him,
to all that call upon him in truth.*

PSALM 145:18

908

*Be still, and know that I am God: I will be exalted
among the heathen, I will be exalted in the earth.*

PSALM 46:10

909

*Thine, O Lord is the greatness, and the power, and the glory,
and the victory, and the majesty: for all that is in the heaven
and in the earth is thine; thine is the kingdom, O Lord,
and thou art exalted as head above all. Both riches and
honour come of thee, and thou reignest over all; and in
thine hand is power and might; and in thine hand it
is to make great, and to give strength unto all.*

1 Chronicles 29:11–12

910

*But I say unto you, Love your enemies, bless them that curse
you, do good to them that hate you, and pray for them which
despitefully use you, and persecute you; that ye may be the
children of your Father which is in heaven: for he maketh
his sun to rise on the evil and on the good,
and sendeth rain on the just and on the unjust.*

Matthew 5:44–45

911

*Through the tender mercy of our God; whereby the
dayspring from on high hath visited us, to give light to
them that sit in darkness and in the shadow of death,
to guide our feet into the way of peace.*

Luke 1:78–79

912

*Verily I say unto you, Wheresoever this gospel shall be
preached throughout the whole world, this also that she
hath done shall be spoken of for a memorial of her.*

MARK 14:9

913

*And his inward affection is more abundant toward
you, whilst he remembereth the obedience of you all,
how with fear and trembling ye received him.*

2 CORINTHIANS 7:15

914

*For our conversation is in heaven; from whence also we look
for the Saviour, the Lord Jesus Christ: who shall change our
vile body, that it may be fashioned like unto his glorious body,
according to the working whereby he is able even
to subdue all things unto himself.*

PHILIPPIANS 3:20–21

915

*But the LORD said unto Samuel, Look not on his countenance,
or on the height of his stature; because I have refused him:
for the LORD seeth not as man seeth; for man looketh on the
outward appearance, but the LORD looketh on the heart.*

1 SAMUEL 16:7

916

Blessed is he that considereth the poor: the LORD will deliver him in time of trouble. The LORD will preserve him, and keep him alive; and he shall be blessed upon the earth: and thou wilt not deliver him unto the will of his enemies.

PSALM 41:1–2

917

Every man also to whom God hath given riches and wealth, and hath given him power to eat thereof, and to take his portion, and to rejoice in his labour; this is the gift of God.

ECCLESIASTES 5:19

918

For every one shall be salted with fire, and every sacrifice shall be salted with salt.

MARK 9:49

919

In my Father's house are many mansions: if it were not so, I would have told you. I go to prepare a place for you. And if I go and prepare a place for you, I will come again, and receive you unto myself; that where I am, there ye may be also.

JOHN 14:2–3

920

He that trusteth in his own heart is a fool: but whoso walketh wisely, he shall be delivered.

PROVERBS 28:26

921

For I will pour water upon him that is thirsty, and floods upon the dry ground: I will pour my spirit upon thy seed, and my blessing upon thine offspring.

ISAIAH 44:3

922

For as a young man marrieth a virgin, so shall thy sons marry thee: and as the bridegroom rejoiceth over the bride, so shall thy God rejoice over thee.

ISAIAH 62:5

923

And said unto them, Whosoever shall receive this child in my name receiveth me: and whosoever shall receive me receiveth him that sent me: for he that is least among you all, the same shall be great.

LUKE 9:48

924

For I will not trust in my bow, neither shall my sword save me. But thou hast saved us from our enemies, and hast put them to shame that hated us.

PSALM 44:6–7

925

Jesus answered and said unto him, If a man love me, he will keep my words: and my Father will love him, and we will come unto him, and make our abode with him.

JOHN 14:23

926

But when Jesus saw it, he was much displeased, and said unto them, Suffer the little children to come unto me, and forbid them not: for of such is the kingdom of God. Verily I say unto you, Whosoever shall not receive the kingdom of God as a little child, he shall not enter therein. And he took them up in his arms, put his hands upon them, and blessed them.

MARK 10:14–16

927

For my name's sake will I defer mine anger, and for my praise will I refrain for thee, that I cut thee not off.

ISAIAH 48:9

928

That they do good, that they be rich in good works, ready to distribute, willing to communicate; laying up in store for themselves a good foundation against the time to come, that they may lay hold on eternal life.

1 TIMOTHY 6:18–19

929

And I heard a voice from heaven saying unto me, Write, Blessed are the dead which die in the Lord from henceforth: Yea, saith the Spirit, that they may rest from their labours; and their works do follow them.

REVELATION 14:13

930

The sleep of a labouring man is sweet, whether he eat little or much: but the abundance of the rich will not suffer him to sleep.

ECCLESIASTES 5:12

931

If they obey and serve him, they shall spend their days in prosperity, and their years in pleasures.

JOB 36:11

932

Declaring the end from the beginning, and from ancient times the things that are not yet done, saying, My counsel shall stand, and I will do all my pleasure.

ISAIAH 46:10

933

He that hath a bountiful eye shall be blessed; for he giveth of his bread to the poor.

PROVERBS 22:9

934

Remember the word unto thy servant, upon which thou hast caused me to hope. This is my comfort in my affliction: for thy word hath quickened me.

PSALM 119:49–50

935

And in that day ye shall ask me nothing. Verily, verily, I say unto you, Whatsoever ye shall ask the Father in my name, he will give it you. Hitherto have ye asked nothing in my name: ask, and ye shall receive, that your joy may be full.

JOHN 16:23–24

936

Now unto him that is able to do exceeding abundantly above all that we ask or think, according to the power that worketh in us, unto him be glory in the church by Christ Jesus throughout all ages, world without end.

EPHESIANS 3:20–21

937

Is not this laid up in store with me, and sealed up among my treasures? To me belongeth vengeance and recompence; their foot shall slide in due time: for the day of their calamity is at hand, and the things that shall come upon them make haste.

DEUTERONOMY 32:34–35

938

And even to your old age I am he; and even to hoar hairs will I carry you: I have made, and I will bear; even I will carry, and will deliver you.

ISAIAH 46:4

939

And there shall be no night there; and they need no candle,
neither light of the sun; for the Lord God giveth them
light: and they shall reign for ever and ever.
REVELATION 22:5

940

Every man according as he purposeth in his heart, so let him give;
not grudgingly, or of necessity: for God loveth a cheerful giver.
2 CORINTHIANS 9:7

941

But the fruit of the Spirit is love, joy, peace, longsuffering,
gentleness, goodness, faith, meekness, temperance:
against such there is no law.
GALATIANS 5:22–23

942

I beseech you therefore, brethren, by the mercies of God, that
ye present your bodies a living sacrifice, holy, acceptable unto
God, which is your reasonable service. And be not conformed
to this world: but be ye transformed by the renewing of
your mind, that ye may prove what is that good,
and acceptable, and perfect, will of God.
ROMANS 12:1–2

943

*Through wisdom is an house builded; and by understanding
it is established: and by knowledge shall the chambers
be filled with all precious and pleasant riches.*
PROVERBS 24:3–4

944

*For ever, O LORD, thy word is settled in heaven.
Thy faithfulness is unto all generations:
thou hast established the earth, and it abideth.*
PSALM 119:89–90

945

*And God is able to make all grace abound toward you;
that ye, always having all sufficiency in all things,
may abound to every good work.*
2 CORINTHIANS 9:8

946

*Therefore are they before the throne of God, and serve him
day and night in his temple: and he that sitteth on the throne
shall dwell among them. They shall hunger no more, neither
thirst any more; neither shall the sun light on them,
nor any heat. For the Lamb which is in the midst of the
throne shall feed them, and shall lead them unto
living fountains of waters: and God shall
wipe away all tears from their eyes.*
REVELATION 7:15–17

947

Set your affection on things above, not on things on the earth.
For ye are dead, and your life is hid with Christ in God.
COLOSSIANS 3:2–3

948

I, even I, am he that blotteth out thy transgressions for mine
own sake, and will not remember thy sins.
ISAIAH 43:25

949

Then said Jesus unto his disciples, If any man will come after
me, let him deny himself, and take up his cross, and follow me.
For whosoever will save his life shall lose it: and whosoever
will lose his life for my sake shall find it.
MATTHEW 16:24–25

950

Being born again, not of corruptible seed, but of incorruptible,
by the word of God, which liveth and abideth for ever.
1 PETER 1:23

951

If ye be reproached for the name of Christ, happy are ye;
for the spirit of glory and of God resteth upon you: on their
part he is evil spoken of, but on your part he is glorified.
1 PETER 4:14

952

*And he said unto me, My grace is sufficient for thee:
for my strength is made perfect in weakness. Most gladly
therefore will I rather glory in my infirmities,
that the power of Christ may rest upon me.*
2 CORINTHIANS 12:9

953

*Fret not thyself because of evil men, neither be thou envious
at the wicked: for there shall be no reward to the evil man;
the candle of the wicked shall be put out.*
PROVERBS 24:19–20

954

*I know that there is no good in them, but for a man to
rejoice, and to do good in his life. And also that every man
should eat and drink, and enjoy the good of
all his labour, it is the gift of God.*
ECCLESIASTES 3:12–13

955

*And I will pray the Father, and he shall give you another
Comforter, that he may abide with you for ever; even the
Spirit of truth; whom the world cannot receive, because it
seeth him not, neither knoweth him: but ye know him;
for he dwelleth with you, and shall be in you.*
JOHN 14:16–17

956

*With good will doing service, as to the Lord, and not to men:
knowing that whatsoever good thing any man doeth, the
same shall he receive of the Lord, whether he be bond or free.*

Ephesians 6:7–8

957

*The Lord lifteth up the meek:
he casteth the wicked down to the ground.*

Psalm 147:6

958

*The Lord preserveth all them that love him: but all the
wicked will he destroy.*

Psalm 145:20

959

*But God, who is rich in mercy, for his great love wherewith
he loved us, even when we were dead in sins, hath quickened
us together with Christ, (by grace ye are saved;) and hath
raised us up together, and made us sit together in heavenly
places in Christ Jesus: that in the ages to come he might
shew the exceeding riches of his grace in his
kindness toward us through Christ Jesus.*

Ephesians 2:4–7

960

Sing, O heavens; and be joyful, O earth; and break forth into singing, O mountains: for the LORD hath comforted his people, and will have mercy upon his afflicted.
ISAIAH 49:13

961

For verily I say unto you, That whosoever shall say unto this mountain, Be thou removed, and be thou cast into the sea; and shall not doubt in his heart, but shall believe that those things which he saith shall come to pass; he shall have whatsoever he saith.
MARK 11:23

962

The LORD will perfect that which concerneth me: thy mercy, O LORD, endureth for ever: forsake not the works of thine own hands.
PSALM 138:8

963

The LORD is far from the wicked: but he heareth the prayer of the righteous.
PROVERBS 15:29

964

And the afflicted people thou wilt save: but thine eyes are upon the haughty, that thou mayest bring them down.
2 SAMUEL 22:28

965

For the word of the Lord is right;
and all his works are done in truth.
Psalm 33:4

966

Blessed are they that keep his testimonies, and that seek him with
the whole heart. They also do no iniquity: they walk in his ways.
Psalm 119:2–3

967

For this cause shall a man leave his father and mother, and
cleave to his wife; and they twain shall be one flesh: so then
they are no more twain, but one flesh. What therefore God
hath joined together, let not man put asunder.
Mark 10:7–9

968

A seed shall serve him;
it shall be accounted to the Lord for a generation.
Psalm 22:30

969

But now, O Lord, thou art our father; we are the clay,
and thou our potter; and we all are the work of thy hand.
Isaiah 64:8

970

And he said unto his disciples, Therefore I say unto you,
Take no thought for your life, what ye shall eat; neither for
the body, what ye shall put on. The life is more than meat,
and the body is more than raiment.

LUKE 12:22–23

971

Now the God of hope fill you with all joy and peace
in believing, that ye may abound in hope,
through the power of the Holy Ghost.

ROMANS 15:13

972

For now we see through a glass, darkly;
but then face to face: now I know in part;
but then shall I know even as also I am known.

1 CORINTHIANS 13:12

973

Thou hast dealt well with thy servant,
O LORD, according unto thy word.

PSALM 119:65

974

But speaking the truth in love, may grow up into him in all things, which is the head, even Christ: from whom the whole body fitly joined together and compacted by that which every joint supplieth, according to the effectual working in the measure of every part, maketh increase of the body unto the edifying of itself in love.
Ephesians 4:15–16

975

That he may incline our hearts unto him, to walk in all his ways, and to keep his commandments, and his statutes, and his judgments, which he commanded our fathers. And let these my words, wherewith I have made supplication before the Lord, be nigh unto the Lord our God day and night, that he maintain the cause of his servant, and the cause of his people Israel at all times, as the matter shall require.
1 Kings 8:58–59

976

For by thee I have run through a troop; and by my God have I leaped over a wall.
Psalm 18:29

977

For all flesh is as grass, and all the glory of man as the flower of grass. The grass withereth, and the flower thereof falleth away: but the word of the Lord endureth for ever. And this is the word which by the gospel is preached unto you.
1 Peter 1:24–25

978

For though he was crucified through weakness, yet he liveth by the power of God. For we also are weak in him, but we shall live with him by the power of God toward you.
2 CORINTHIANS 13:4

979

But they which shall be accounted worthy to obtain that world, and the resurrection from the dead, neither marry, nor are given in marriage: neither can they die any more: for they are equal unto the angels; and are the children of God, being the children of the resurrection.
LUKE 20:35–36

980

Good and upright is the LORD: therefore will he teach sinners in the way.
PSALM 25:8

981

And when ye stand praying, forgive, if ye have ought against any: that your Father also which is in heaven may forgive you your trespasses.
MARK 11:25

982

Come unto me, all ye that labour and are heavy laden, and I will give you rest. Take my yoke upon you, and learn of me; for I am meek and lowly in heart: and ye shall find rest unto your souls.
MATTHEW 11:28–29

983

A man's heart deviseth his way: but the LORD directeth his steps.
PROVERBS 16:9

984

Calling a ravenous bird from the east, the man that executeth
my counsel from a far country: yea, I have spoken it, I will
also bring it to pass; I have purposed it, I will also do it.
ISAIAH 46:11

985

The words of the LORD are pure words: as silver tried
in a furnace of earth, purified seven times.
PSALM 12:6

986

But the Comforter, which is the Holy Ghost, whom the
Father will send in my name, he shall teach you all things,
and bring all things to your remembrance,
whatsoever I have said unto you.
JOHN 14:26

987

For we are saved by hope: but hope that is seen is not hope: for
what a man seeth, why doth he yet hope for? But if we hope
for that we see not, then do we with patience wait for it.
ROMANS 8:24–25

988

Finally, brethren, farewell. Be perfect, be of good comfort,
be of one mind, live in peace; and the God of
love and peace shall be with you.

2 CORINTHIANS 13:11

989

And, behold, this day I am going the way of all the earth:
and ye know in all your hearts and in all your souls, that not
one thing hath failed of all the good things which the LORD
your God spake concerning you; all are come to pass
unto you, and not one thing hath failed thereof.

JOSHUA 23:14

990

Surely he hath borne our griefs, and carried our sorrows:
yet we did esteem him stricken, smitten of God, and afflicted.

ISAIAH 53:4

991

Whether Paul, or Apollos, or Cephas, or the world, or life,
or death, or things present, or things to come; all are
your's; and ye are Christ's; and Christ is God's.

1 CORINTHIANS 3:22–23

992

Therefore if thine enemy hunger, feed him; if he thirst, give
him drink: for in so doing thou shalt heap coals of fire on his
head. Be not overcome of evil, but overcome evil with good.

ROMANS 12:20–21

993

Therefore my people shall know my name: therefore they shall know in that day that I am he that doth speak: behold, it is I.
ISAIAH 52:6

994

And ye shall be hated of all men for my name's sake: but he that shall endure unto the end, the same shall be saved.
MARK 13:13

995

Therefore, my beloved brethren, be ye stedfast, unmoveable, always abounding in the work of the Lord, forasmuch as ye know that your labour is not in vain in the Lord.
1 CORINTHIANS 15:58

996

And they that know thy name will put their trust in thee: for thou, LORD, hast not forsaken them that seek thee.
PSALM 9:10

997

And they shall build houses, and inhabit them; and they shall plant vineyards, and eat the fruit of them. They shall not build, and another inhabit; they shall not plant, and another eat: for as the days of a tree are the days of my people, and mine elect shall long enjoy the work of their hands.
ISAIAH 65:21–22

998

Who his own self bare our sins in his own body on the tree, that we, being dead to sins, should live unto righteousness: by whose stripes ye were healed.

1 Peter 2:24

999

And if Christ be in you, the body is dead because of sin; but the Spirit is life because of righteousness.

Romans 8:10

1,000

And when I saw him, I fell at his feet as dead. And he laid his right hand upon me, saying unto me, Fear not; I am the first and the last. . .

Revelation 1:17

1,001

Now unto him that is able to keep you from falling, and to present you faultless before the presence of his glory with exceeding joy, to the only wise God our Saviour, be glory and majesty, dominion and power, both now and ever. Amen.

Jude 24–25